D0403849

Aviva-No

NO LONGER PROPERTY OF
THE SEATTLE PUBLIC LIBRARY

Aviva-No

SHIMON ADAF

Translated from the Hebrew by YAEL SEGALOVITZ

Alice James Books
FARMINGTON, MAINE
alicejamesbooks.org

© 2019 by Shimon Adaf
All rights reserved
Printed in the United States

10 9 8 7 6 5 4 3 2 1

Alice James Books are published by Alice James Poetry Cooperative, Inc.,
an affiliate of the University of Maine at Farmington.

Alice James Books
114 Prescott Street
Farmington, ME 04938
www.alicejamesbooks.org

Library of Congress Cataloging-in-Publication Data

Names: Adaf, Shimon, author. | Segalovitz, Yael, translator. | Adaf, Shimon. Aviva-no. English. | Adaf, Shimon, Aviva-no.
Title: Aviva-no / Shimon Adaf ; translated from Hebrew by Yael Segalovitz.
Description: Farmington, Maine : Alice James Books, 2019. | In English with original Hebrew text.
Identifiers: LCCN 2019012545 (print) | LCCN 2019013012 (ebook) | ISBN 9781948579612 (eBook) | ISBN 9781948579056 (pbk. : alk. paper)
Classification: LCC PJ5055.2.D44 (ebook) | LCC PJ5055.2.D44 A9613 2019 (print) | DDC 892.41/7--dc23
LC record available at https://lccn.loc.gov/2019012545

Alice James Books gratefully acknowledges support from individual donors, private foundations, the University of Maine at Farmington, the National Endowment for the Arts, and the Amazon Literary Partnership.

Supported by: Am Ha-Sefer, The Israeli Fund for Translation of Hebrew Books, The Cultural Administration, Israel Ministry of Culture and Sport, and The Rabinovich Foundation for the Arts.

Originally published in Hebrew by Dvir, 2009, and published in this volume courtesy of Dvir and in arrangement with The Institute for The Translation of Hebrew Literature.

Cover art: "Rosh Hanikra" by Erez Segalovitz

Contents

Introduction 1

Whose time is it

I'm in a state of how does it go and I shall call it Aviva-no
I shall call it sisterless 12
At night the destroyers are given permission, 14
They all saw the signs and did not say, 16
I needed the body as well 20
And I did not know that I would have to live 22
She had a heart heavier than the ocean 24
What were your words 26
With what else should I praise thee, Lord,
when I have praised with a rose's tap, with a cascade 28
At the dawn of *Kislev* 32
The residents discovered the bougainvillea: slender necks, quivering 36
Salvation and fear turned into thorns— 38
Shevat crept in coils of ice, cracks 40
The sun—an old man falls asleep in the sun; the light, 44
Where are you? Under a pillow I laid a book 46

Clangs on the anvil of light

Let me have those shapes that shrivel language 50
What is wrong with them, the mustard plants,
that they are irritated thus all of a sudden, 52
And I once already learned 56
But if compelled to give form to 58
One can sing of rain, the mightiness 60
A stretched glimmer is the glass 64
The body knew what it knew 68
I recall the flame tree made taut with summer 74
Fine as sea amidst a summered winter 78
Noooooo, pain, don't let go—my heart, don't cease in sorrow, 82
Here you are. Revealed to me molded in the flesh 84
Forty-three years old, you are the woman you will always be. 88
Her laughter, even a twitch of the lip, the weight 90
Just before I fell asleep I think 92

It was once already

We were sentenced to be haunted all our days by the tree of the Jews, 96
The sons' lot the same as 98
(Who would we have been if not dispersed, people 100
So where is the gate 102
For years I had this somber velvet 104
In the year nineteen eighty-seven 108
Pillars of thistle in the storm's electric bright 112
For one day I will desert that city-far-off, 114
Sex and loneliness and coals 116
Like lovers who house-warmed by fucking 118
Sderot is clenched in winter, a radiance of cotton caresses 120
I'll probably lose my mind, this dick just doesn't hold 122
Orchid, a tree, perhaps 126
This poem is not fit for music, it reaches from afar, 128

A psalm for Tamar may you be saved from the ashes 134

This translation is dedicated with gratitude to
Robert Alter and Taylor Johnston

"How Will I Speak Her?": A Critical Introduction to Aviva-No *by Yael Segalovitz*

"Elegy presents every thing as lost and gone, or absent and future."
—Samuel Taylor Coleridge

My first encounter with *Aviva-No*—the third and most recent poetry collection of the acclaimed Israeli author, Shimon Adaf—was of a mystical, or better yet a ghostly, nature. In entering a bookstore in Tel Aviv, a new slim book on the display table immediately caught my eye. There was nothing conspicuous about it; in fact, its appearance was quite underwhelming—a black cover and on it, a sandy-brown rectangle surrounding a dark title: *Aviva-No*. But emanating from this gravestone-like cover, and from the pages behind it, were aching voices: Aviva is no longer; Aviva, a presence in negation; Aviva, I pray, don't. Indeed, as I quickly learned, *Aviva-No* is a haunting, strikingly beautiful elegy that gives no solace to its bewitched reader. It pains, mourns, refuses to fathom, and desperately tries to articulate via its rich and inventive Hebrew, the loss of Aviva, Adaf's older sister, and by extension "every thing" that is "lost and gone," in Coleridge's words above.

Seldom in the history of elegy do we find the sister to be the object of lament, the one whose absence renders everything at once "absent and future." When women figures do enter the genre, they commonly take the form of a nymph, a muse, or an abstract metaphor (recall Wera Knoop in Rilke's *Sonnets to Orpheus*).[1] Yet in *Aviva-No*, it is the death of the flesh and blood Aviva ("Forty-three years old, you are the woman you will always be"), which brings the world into utter collapse: "the whole world has broken so, facing Aviva-no." Adaf not only spares Aviva the stereotypical role of the goddess of inspiration; he presents her as the very intellectual who introduced the speaker of *Aviva-No*, and perhaps the poet himself, to the world of letters and literary art—"And here you set me down, showed me / the books"—a role reserved in the patriarchal tradition for masculine father figures.

Alongside Aviva, Adaf's cycle of poems finds another protagonist, the Hebrew language itself. Adaf's speaker, with his blazing grief, melts the Hebrew down only to then remold it into previously unknown forms. It is thus that in poem 13, "light" in its radiation "*entifies* objects", and in poem 3, the ghosts of the dead are said to have "feared *at*" the speaker. In the same vein, the overbearing heat that arises from Adaf's poems allows him to fuse together Hebrew words from distant semantic realms in order to accomplish the impossible task of putting loss into words. The speaker's body is depicted, in the poem that opens the second section of the collection, as being *mushar*, "word by word". *Mushar* does not exist as a verb in Hebrew, but it grammatically makes sense to the reader as the passive participle of either the verb "to sing" (from the root sh.i.r) or of the verb "to cast off" (as in a tree shedding its leaves, from the root n.sh.r). This linguistic deformation works to conjure an emphatic image: the speaker's body appears as an entity that is slowly, "word by word," decomposing itself, while also triggering, precisely through this process of decay, the creation of "song," a term that in Hebrew refers both to poetry and to music.

Paradoxically, this linguistic flexibility, which the speaker finds in Hebrew, and which enables him to articulate Aviva's death, also sets off his rage against the language. He depicts Hebrew words, in poem 15, as "malicious sluts [who] say Aviva is gone" by lending themselves a vehicle for this dreadful news. By way of revenge, the speaker swears to "lay bare [the words'] roots, / their evil-doings I shall dash against the stone..." This line alludes to the horrible concluding image of Psalms 137. The psalm famously opens with the mourners—the Israelite captives, exiled from Jerusalem by the Babylonians—as they express their sorrow via song, very much like Adaf's speaker: "By the rivers of Babylon,

[1] Scholarship presents a complex picture of the role women play in the genre of elegy. On the one hand, articles such as Celeste M. Schenck's seminal "Feminism and Deconstruction: Re-Constructing the Elegy" emphasize the patriarchal thrust of the genre. She writes, "The funeral elegy is, from its inception in the poetry of Theocritus and his followers, Bion and Moschus, a resolutely patriarchal genre... it is modelled on archaic initiation rituals of [a] younger man by an elder" (*Tulsa Studies in Women's Literature* 5, no. 1 [1986], 13). On the other hand, critics such as Gail Holst-Warhaft trace women as makers and performers of lament to classical Greece (*Dangerous Voices: Women's Laments and Greek Literature* [London & New York: Routledge, 1992]). In *Aviva-No*, Adaf considers the two facets of the genre. As I will discuss below, he reacts against the patriarchal formula of elegy through the queering of gender and sex, and, in the spirit of Holst-Warhaft, evokes the ancient role of women as professional lamenters, specifically in the Middle Eastern tradition.

there we sat down, yea, we wept, when we remembered Zion" (KJV).[2] But Adaf points not to this opening melancholic image but to the violent one which brings the psalm to a close, depicting the Israelites' vengeful rage against their captives: "daughter of Babylon the despoiler, happy who pays you back in kind, for what you did to us. Happy who seizes and smashes your infants against the rock" (RA). In *Aviva-No*, rage is directed at Hebrew itself, the language that functions as the condition of possibility for the expression of the speaker's pain. That is, within the poetic universe of *Aviva-No*, Hebrew is the agent of both destruction and reconstruction. I will return to poem 15 below, but for now suffice it to say that this unique combination gives the collection its avant-garde form and allows it to mourn the dead while, in the same throbbing breath, renewing language.

Aviva-No's poignant expression of personal loss nevertheless makes an important intervention in a much larger Israeli cultural and political conversation that holds global relevance. This may very well be related to Adaf's own biography, which encapsulates and brings into stark relief the most intractable conflicts underlying Israeli identity politics today. Adaf is a son of Moroccan immigrants, who have historically been grouped in Israeli culture (together with immigrants from other North African and Middle Eastern communities) under the rubric of "Mizrachi" ("Eastern") Jews. The Mizrachi rebellion against their long-lasting, systematic exclusion from the Israeli cultural and political mainstream reached a fever pitch in the last decade, expressed, among other developments, by the establishment of an ambitious young coterie of poets—named "Ars-Poetica"—who raise the banner of the Mizrachi struggle in their work.[3] Adaf, for his part, takes a different stance within this struggle. Undoubtedly, his Moroccan upbringing and Mizrachi roots are strewn across *Aviva-No*. To mention just one example out of many, Adaf invokes the longstanding Middle-Eastern tradition, mentioned already in the Book of Jeremiah (9:17), of looking to women for the production and performance of lament, in an effort to unsettle the abovementioned elegiac patriarchal formula. For that reason, as early as the second poem, Adaf portrays three women, three sisters to be exact, as the ones who try to sew together the texture—and text—of Aviva's body, and her loss: "The remaining sisters sit and sew / the shreds of the rent body." But Adaf's identification with and reliance on Mizrachi Middle-Eastern tradition never takes the form of an explicit and generalized statement, neither in *Aviva-No* nor in the other works that comprise his oeuvre. In his mind, the resistance to naming—to raising any banner whatsoever—is itself a political move, a possible reason for his reluctance to publicly align himself with

[2] I have used throughout either the King James or Robert Alter's translation of the Bible, here marked as KJV and RA, respectively.
[3] The group's name is a wordplay in Hebrew, alluding to Horace's *The Art of Poetry* while also reappropriating the derogatory term "ars", "pimp" in Arabic, which in the Israeli context is stereotypically associated with Mizrachi men. Important to note that Ars Poetica did not yet exist when *Aviva-No* was written, thus that Adaf's dialogue in this collection is with Ars Poetica's influential (yet too frequently unmentioned) precursors, such as Sami Shalom Chetrit, Mois Benarroch, Vicki Shiran, and Shelley Elkayam.

"Ars-Poetica." As he writes in his recent essay, "The I Who Desires to Declare I":[4]

> Once and again I pause in front of trees, the light arrested in their branches during certain hours of the day, in certain seasons. At times, other sights demand my presence, demand that I attend. A bird cutting through the air, the movement of shade, a countenance, a bodily gesture, eyes, the accent of people I loved which embodies endless warmth, customs and manners that form my very neural network, the cells that shape my veins... Even "Moroccanness" is too general a term for this claim made upon me... even "My Moroccanness" is an empty vessel. This claim has no name but the singular one I give it each time anew.[5]

There is no point, then, in searching for an overt invocation of Adaf's Mizrachi identity in *Aviva-No*. Instead, the contours of his singular experience of being in the world—structured by, yet surpassing the label "Moroccanness"—lie among the bougainvillea, almond trees, loam sandstones, hibiscus bushes, balsam trees, warblers, flame trees, crows, or asphalt lines that pave the imagined though profoundly Israeli landscape of *Aviva-No*.[6]

Adaf also conveys his Mizrachi background in *Aviva-No* via his ongoing dialogue with traditional Jewish texts and praxes. In the Israeli context, Mizrachi culture is historically associated with an intimate affinity for Jewish tradition that is not restricted to and by Jewish Law (a religious stance usually referred to as *masorti'ut*). Adaf was raised in an orthodox household, where, though his mother and father adhered to very different conceptions of the Jewish faith, they both encouraged him to acquire an in-depth Jewish education. His father especially hoped for him to become a rabbi and provided him with the required rigorous education. Adaf ended up veering away from this path, yet his multilingual knowledge of the Jewish sources reverberates throughout his work, from the Hebrew Bible, through the Aramaic Mishna and Talmud, all the way to the Jewish prayer book (this is especially true of Adaf's trilogy *Nuntia* [2010], *Mox Nox* [2011], and *De Urbibus Infenis* [2012]). In *Aviva-No* specifically, Adaf enters into dialogue with Jewish tradition through his repeated, and furious, addresses to God. Adaf's speaker does not denounce God for the calamity that befell his family. Instead, in the spirit of Job or Jonah, he directs his fury at God, as in poem 7: "What were your words / to my sister / in the bathroom [...] He who sticks His blazing wrath / into mortal affairs, / with Your barren

---

[4] Shimon Adaf, "The I Who Desires to Declare I", in *I am Others* (Be'er Sheva: Kinneret, Zmora-Bitan, Dvir & Heksherim Institute, 2018), 9-19. All unattributed translations are mine.

[5] Ibid., 14.

[6] For an interesting exploration of Adaf's interaction with Mizrachi culture via multicultural poetic language, see Dorit Lemberger, "Questioning Boundaries of Language and the World: Ambivalence and Disillusionment in the Writings of Shimon Adaf," *Hebrew Studies* 56, no. 1 (2015): 265-294.

silence, in this morning / of unbearable pain, / You, / tell me –." In the following poem, number 8, Adaf's speaker forcefully accuses God of taking pleasure in death and in the unique form of address to the divine it elicits: "who else has praised thee thus / [...] with a sister, with her fleeting breath in the bathroom, with a / conquered heart and with flesh lying on the floor, turning blue, / bursting with a splendor of eternal silence, with a mother desperately kissing it / Who had once lauded thee." At the same time, Adaf remains critical of institutionalized religion, portraying, for instance, a rabbi who explains away Aviva's death with the simplistic theological argument: "a guardian angel [...] She is saving a foreign cousin / from being impaled on an iron pole." In the same vein, he also sarcastically depicts a "wise man" who enters the mourners' house and "orders": "donate to / the synagogue."

However, what is most striking in Adaf's engagement with the Jewish sources in *Aviva-No* is his frequent gestures toward Jewish mourning rituals, particularly esoteric ones, whose significance is for the most part lost on its practitioners. These idiosyncratic practices permit *Aviva-No* to communicate the mourners' collapse of sensemaking in the face of loss. Such, for instance, is the ritual of reading during the *shiv'ah* (the seven days of mourning) the Mishnaic text "Stoking the Incense" (*pitum ha-ketoret*), which details the 365 ingredients that were required to light the incense offering in the Holy Temple of Jerusalem. "Pitum ha-ketoret" reads like a secret recipe, containing names of ingredients whose meaning has been lost over time, and meticulously regulating a ritual that has long disappeared from existence.[7] This enigmatic text, which some even believe holds mystical powers, makes its entrance already in *Aviva-No*'s first poem, which concludes: "and the heart is arrested and named mere breath / for the three hundred and sixty five minas of smoke within it / against the count of three hundred and sixty five days of." This final line lingers on the tongue in its uncanny unconcluded form ("days *of*"), mimicking the abrupt cessation of Aviva's life. Yet by gesturing towards this Mishnaic portion, Adaf also highlights the Jewish ritual's role—precisely due to its unintelligibility—in helping the mourner to cope with a time out of joint, and engage in the labor of sewing the 365 days of the year back together, even if this labor is doomed to fail. After all, the fictional time depicted in the collection is spread over one year exactly (the Jewish year of mourning), opening and closing with the Hebrew month of *Kislev* in which the death took place, and in between following the months of the Jewish calendar ("*Shevat* crept in coils of ice," "*Adar* unfolds in melded skies," "the heavy heat of *Tammuz*," "[a] broiling *Av*").

For Haviva Pedaya, a prominent Mizrachi Israeli poet and scholar, Adaf's engagement with esoteric Jewish texts has a strong political valence. In referring to Adaf's

[7] *Pitum ha-ketoret* is said by the practicing Jew several times a day, every day. However, it receives special status during the *shiv'ah*, when it is read in the mourners' house.

intertextual dialogue with "*pitum ha-ketoret*," she writes:

> In the context of Israeli culture, a Mizrachi child frequently finds himself laboring to comprehend the full meaning of a cultural object, which perhaps captivates him with its beauty, but also pushes him away since he lacks the tools needed to decode it. Why shouldn't the center stand thus facing the periphery [...] and labor to understand its opaqueness? What is peripheral here [in *Aviva-No*], you ask? The endlessly layered language that was submerged [in Israel] under one flattened Hebrew.[8]

Pedaya configures together cultural and geographical exclusion. She links the cultural peripheralization of the "endlessly layered" Hebrew that Mizrachi tradition preserves in its unique affinity for Jewish tradition, with the geographic peripheralization of Mizrachi Jews (The "periphery" is colloquial Hebrew for the predominantly Mizrachi under-privileged areas, especially in the south of the country). And indeed, *Aviva-No* takes place in the Israeli geo-cultural outskirts, more specifically, in the terror-stricken Gaza-bordering city of Sderot, where Adaf grew up, and where his speaker bemoans Aviva.

As the target of dozens of rockets since the second Palestinian intifada (September 2000), Sderot has become one of the most prevalent symbols in the Israeli imaginary for the devastating Israeli-Palestinian conflict. It is not surprising, then, to find that "*Qassam* rockets," "bomb shelters," and the "Gaza Strip" recur throughout *Aviva-No*. Yet here as well, Adaf refuses to fight any one-sided battle. He will not emphasize the suffering on one side of the border at the expense of the other. As he writes in poem 32, "So where is the gate / in Gaza, in Sderot – // The underworld of former times; the air / still faint / and we go through." The "underworld" in *Aviva-No* extends its hellish existence over the two sides of the border, a territory scorched by political forces blind to human misery "in Gaza, in Sderot." Within this earthly inferno, even natural beauty is out of reach: "Orchid, a tree, perhaps / only a bush, and still, a verdant vessel / seizing voices that *Nissan* / threatens to eject: a stamen – a caw of color, a petal – / a howl of hue. / This is all in reach, that is, / unreachable, in Gaza, in Sderot, / an enthralled *Adar* is swarming" (poem 41). In the same vein, Adaf insists throughout the collection on bringing to the fore the frequently silenced presence of Arabic in the Hebrew language, in Jewish history, and in the mouths of Palestinians and Arab-Israelis within the Israeli public sphere. Adaf compels his reader to recall both the intimate link between Mizrachi and Arab cultures, and the long-standing historical dialogue between Jewish and Arabic-speaking communities and literatures. In poem 25, for example, he writes: "and the neighbor

[8] Haviva Pedaya, "*Aviva-No* by Shimon Adaf: Not by Way of Verse but by Pain" ["יפל אלא הרישה דרד לע אל :ידא ונעמש תאמ אל-הביבא באכ"], *Ha'aretz*, March 24, 2010. https://www.haaretz.co.il/literature/poetry/1.1194518.

rants unaware in Arabic / *Wu'natalti ruha u'shmait batrai kal zia sagi* –". In this line, Adaf deftly mobilizes the orthographic similarity between the Hebrew term for Arabic (*Aravit*) and the name of the Jewish evening prayer service (*Arvit*), making the neighbor rant "in Arabic" Aramaic words from the Jewish prayer "And a Redeemer Shall Come to Zion".[9] In this way, Adaf underscores the close affinity between Arab and Jewish traditions. Even more provocatively, through this linguistic manipulation, he is able to lure the reader, especially the secular one unacquainted with the Jewish prayer book, into believing that the neighbor's Aramaic prayer *is* indeed a "rant" in Arabic, thus revealing how Aramaic and Arabic are similarly foreign to the contemporary ear. All this is astutely done without ceasing to summon Aviva. After all, the sentence Adaf quotes from "And a Redeemer Shall Come to Zion" conjures precisely the figure of the ghost: "then a spirit [also, ghost] carried me away, and behind me I heard a great roaring sound".

Adaf, then, has a foot in both *Mizrachi* and *Ashkenazi* (stereotypically construed as "Eastern" and "Western") identities, religious and secular thought, and, to a certain degree, Jewish and Arab cultures, the three binaries that set the parameters of contemporary Israeli socio-political discourse. Adaf adamantly resists adhering to any stable identity on these three continuums, since, as he further writes in "The I Who Desires to Declare I": "In our times, the field of representations is replete with invitations to… endlessly speak out one's identity, to make it easily distinguishable from the other endless array of possibilities presented to the individual, so that one could stop and say: I'm an A and a B and a C, with a bit of D on the side."[10] The result, he warns, is that

> self-definition [is] achieved through constant identification with a certain identity category. Consequently, all internal efforts are directed at consolidating that identity category, sealing its cracks and fissures, differentiating it from other [identity] categories, which are then perceived, as a result of the effort to entrench oneself in one's category, as hostile. Thus, the core of identity politics as it is practiced in everyday discourse is sameness and not otherness, a desire towards identification. [11]

At the heart of *Aviva-No* is a subjectivity that teeters on the edge of the abyss, of utter collapse in the face of loss ("I ceased to see / how I shall live / life anymore / what of"). This driving disintegrating force makes Adaf's continuous battle against "sameness" even more pronounced in this work than in his oeuvre more generally. As I've observed, Adaf resists any easy "identification" in *Aviva-No* by unsettling the narrow, stable categories through

---

[9] "And a Redeemer Shall Come to Zion" is said during the evening prayer (*Aravit*) on Saturdays and during special occasions such as the fast day of *Tisha B'Av*, and the holiday of *Purim*.
[10] Adaf, "The I Who Desires to Say I," 9.
[11] Ibid., 12.

which his poetry is in danger of being understood when read against the backdrop of his biography. He also consistently, systematically, and ingeniously defamiliarizes Hebrew through his elegiac poetry, making it foreign even, and perhaps especially, to its native speakers. Yet, as one would expect from a poet dedicated to otherness, Adaf takes another, unexpected route in destabilizing a consolidated identity. He does this by queering both gender and sex, placing his speaker, his reader, and even Hebrew itself in an imaginary body that refuses the confines of the imposed rigid categories masculine vs. feminine, man vs. woman.

As we recall, in poem 15, Adaf compares Hebrew words to "sluts" (whose babies the enraged speaker craves to "dash against the stones") in the spirit of the biblical revenge against the Babylonians. This poem, then, begins by presenting Hebrew as a woman in an overdetermined fashion; it does so in metaphorical figuration ("slut," mother), through its intertextual dialogue (Hebrew is the equivalent of the "daughter of Babylon the despoiler"), and by highlighting grammatical gender as a sight of personification ("language" is grammatically feminine in Hebrew).[12] In this way, the readers are led to infer that the speaker who refers to Hebrew as a "slut" and evokes the biblical misogynist scene (in which the Israelite male captives imagine punishing the Babylonian daughters for their fathers' violence) is a man. But the poem's second half subverts and unsettles its own established gender hierarchy. The speaker states "malicious sluts say Aviva is gone. / But I was / as well, Hebrew pounding on / my throat-bell, I answered aye. / It has the dick of a camel, that one." We learn that the ostensibly male speaker of the poem, who invoked the "malicious sluts," confesses "I was, as well," leaving us to wonder: Is s/he a slut too? This question is dragged over to the next line, where a sexualized image presents Hebrew, supposedly a metaphorical woman, as the one doing the "pounding" with the speaker, who voluntarily participates ("I answered aye"). In this way, the simple binaries of passive/active and penetrating/penetrated are profoundly destabilized. This deconstruction reaches a crescendo in the final line, where Adaf's gender-sex provocation is necessarily lost in translation. The original Hebrew reads: "*She* has the dick of a camel, that one". The "she" in the original refers to the grammatically feminine Hebrew language, in this way foregrounding the question of gender and sex. Adaf leverages the fact that Hebrew is an exceedingly gendered language in order to boldly flaunt its intersexed figuration. Put bluntly, Adaf's Hebrew is a "she" with a "dick," and his male mourner is a "slut" being "pounded." In Adaf's universe, then, the very body of language evades "sameness," allowing him to impart fluidity to formal structures and identity categories.

[12] In this sense, Adaf participates in this poem in the destabilization of the pivotal metaphor of the land/city as a woman, which runs like a thread through Hebrew literature from the Bible to the present. This metaphorical system with its literary and political implications is the subject of Chana Kronfeld's book project, *The Land as Woman: The Afterlife of a Poetic Metaphor in Women's Modern Hebrew Poetry* (in preparation).

To come full circle, the effort of translating *Aviva-No* entailed a prolonged listening to and lingering with the collection's singular, haunting, poetic voices. However, like any ghostly utterance, these voices turned out to be difficult, if not impossible, to grasp and make legible in English; this was the case especially since, in contrast with Hebrew, English does not gender nouns, a trait of which Adaf makes extensive and crafty use. Moreover, Adaf's intense dialogue with Jewish sources and his multilingual play do not allow for an easy transition into a different linguistic realm. This is particularly felt in poem 28, where Adaf transcribes English in Hebrew letters, mimicking the Hebrew speaker's accent and common mistakes in what is considered in Israel the language of prestige. What I nevertheless labored to preserve at any cost was the emotional intensity of Adaf's experimental poetry, by resisting the temptation to smooth over *Aviva-No*'s unique and defamiliarizing texture, syntax, and structure. *Aviva-No* is a seismographic text, charting in its vibrating language the tectonic, transformative pain that erupts and consumes one's being in the face of death. My hope is that the readers of this translation will be able to feel these seismic waves pulsating under Adaf's words.

—*Yael Segalovitz,* May 2019

Whose time is it
like metal, retaining cold
and lightning.

And why should I live it,
weighing on the chest
any attempt to escape
will rupture the aorta.

(Object, 1)

שֶׁל מִי הַזְּמַן הַזֶּה
כְּמוֹ מַתְּכוֹת, צוֹבֵר הַקֹּר
וְהַבְּרָקִים.

וְלָמָּה שֶׁאֶחְיֶה אוֹתוֹ,
מֶנַח עַל הֶחָזֶה
כָּל נִסְיוֹן מִלּוּט
יִקְרַע אֶת אַב הָעוֹרְקִים.

(דְּבָר, 1)

1.

I'm in a state of how does it go and I shall call it Aviva-no I shall call it sisterless
and I shall speak of it with straightforwardness not by way of verse but by pain
and thus is its Law it has no Law—stifling-breath angels and blazing-eyed
beasts, in the internet above and the buried books below, it has no
Law, it is only the moment piercing space like a pin into glass
and the heart is arrested and named mere breath
for the three hundred and sixty-five minas of smoke within it
against the count of three hundred and sixty-five days of.

א.

אֲנִי בְּמַצָּב אֵיךְ לְהַגְדִּירוֹ וְאֶקְרָאֵהוּ אֲבִיבָה־לֹא אֶקְרָאֵהוּ אֵינָּחוֹת
וַאֲדַבְּרָה בּוֹ יְשִׁירוֹת לֹא עַל דֶּרֶךְ הַשִּׁירָה אֶלָּא לְפִי כְּאֵב
וְזֹאת הִיא תּוֹרָתוֹ אֵין לוֹ תּוֹרָה – מַלְאָכִים מְחַנְּקִים נְשִׁימָה וְחַיּוֹת
בּוֹעֲרוֹת עֵינַיִם, בָּאִינְטֶרְנֶט מִמַּעַל וּבַסְּפָרִים הַנִּקְבָּרִים, אֵין
לוֹ תּוֹרָה, רַק הָרֶגַע בְּעָצְמוֹת הֶחָלָל הוּא נוֹקֵב כְּסֻכָּה בִּזְכוּכִית
וְהַלֵּב הֶחָדוּל וְקָרוּי הֶבֶל
מִשּׁוּם שְׁלוֹשׁ מֵאוֹת שִׁשִּׁים וַחֲמִשָּׁה מָנִים שֶׁל עָשָׁן שֶׁבּוֹ
כְּנֶגֶד שְׁלוֹשׁ מֵאוֹת שִׁשִּׁים וַחֲמִשָּׁה מִנְיַן יְמוֹת.

2.

At night the destroyers are given permission,
the flaming vault of heavens, merciless. Downcast *Kislev*,
a black conflagration is within him.

The remaining sisters sit and sew
the shreds of the rent body.
One threads a string, the other
strikes the needle,
the third screams, oh no!
the finger, it is pricked.

Blinders of the moons, a sketch in silver
fine as cracked skin, and the fire
of the crimson drop is glowing.

Blood moves in the world yet suffices not for one being
to be saved
and blood spills, how to put it,
fountains and depths spring out
of valleys and hills.

ב.

לַיְלָה רָשׁוּת לַמְּחַבְּלִים הוּא,
לַהַט רְקִיעִים עָרֵל. כִּסְלֵו הַסָּר יֵשׁ
לוֹ תַּבְעֵרָה שְׁחֹרָה.

יוֹשְׁבוֹת וּמַטְלִיאוֹת הָאֲחָיוֹת הַנּוֹתָרוֹת
מְקוֹם קְרִיעַת הַגּוּף.
אַחַת מַשְׁחֶלֶת חוּט, שְׁנִיָּה
מַכָּה בַּמַּחַט,
שְׁלִישִׁית צוֹוַחַת: אָח,
הָאֶצְבַּע, הִיא דֶּקֶרָה.

סַךְ הַסְּהָרִים שִׁרְטוּט שֶׁל כֶּסֶף
דַּק כְּמוֹ עוֹר נִבְקָע וְאֵשׁ
הָאַרְגָּמָן שֶׁל הַטִּפָּה זוֹרֵחַ.

דָּם זָז בָּעוֹלָם וְלֹא מַסְפִּיק לְנֶפֶשׁ
אֵין דַּי לְהַצִּיל
וְדָם זָז, אֵיךְ לוֹמַר,
תְּהוֹם וַעֲיָנוֹת יוֹצְאִים
בָּעֵמֶק וּבָהָר.

3.

They all saw the signs and did not say,
but my mother spoke of her vision
a week before: deceased family
gather at the door,
trudge to the bedroom, ghostly faces
mourn with her. As for me, all those I invented
came back from the dead. On the sea shore
they feared at me, in the poisoned glare
of heavens' vault against electric light, in roiled
curtains near an oleander thicket, in a flock of nightingales,
in the halls, in soul-corrupting blogs.

Later, dreams, and not mine:
Light, rare, washing the living room,
a stranger in jeans and a T-shirt unbinds
my sister's throat. A guardian angel, explains the Rabbi.
She is saving a foreign cousin
from being impaled on an iron pole. Donate to
the synagogue, another wise man orders. Leaving,
a bag on her back, if only she
commanded, you go to your lives, we

ג.

לְכֻלָּם הָיוּ אוֹתוֹתֵיהֶם שֶׁלָּם וְלֹא אָמְרוּ
אֲבָל אִמִּי סִפְּרָה אֵיךְ רָאֲתָה
שָׁבוּעַ קֹדֶם: בְּנֵי מִשְׁפַּחְתָּהּ
הַמְּנוֹחִים נֶאֱסָפִים לַדֶּלֶת
וּמִשְׁתָּרְכִים לְחֶדֶר הַשֵּׁנָה, פְּנֵי רְפָאִים
נָדִים לָהּ. אֲנִי כָּל מִי שֶׁבָּדִיתִי
חָזַר מִן הַמֵּתִים. עַל חוֹף הַיָּם
הָיָה פַּחְדָּם אֵלַי, בַּבֹּהַק הַמֶּרְעָל שֶׁל
רְקִיעִים כְּנֶגֶד תְּאוּרַת חַשְׁמַל, בְּוִילָאוֹת
סוֹעִים סָמוּךְ לִסְבַךְ הַרְדּוּף, בְּלַהַק זְמִירִים,
בַּפְּרוֹזְדוֹרִים, בַּבְּלוּגִים מַדִּיחֵי הַנֶּפֶשׁ.

אַחַר כָּךְ חֲלוֹמוֹת, וְלֹא שֶׁלִּי:
אוֹר־אֵין־בִּלְתּוֹ שׁוֹטֵף אֶת הַסָּלוֹן,
גֶּבֶר זָר בְּגִ׳ינְס וּבִטְרִיקוֹ מַתִּיר גְּרוֹנָהּ
שֶׁל אֲחוֹתִי. מַלְאָךְ שׁוֹמֵר, מַבְהִיר הָרַב.
הִיא מַצִּילָה בַּת דּוֹדָה רְחוֹקָה
מֵהִשְׁתַּפְּדוּת עַל מוֹט בַּרְזֶל. לִתְרֹם לְבֵית
הַכְּנֶסֶת, פּוֹקֵד חָכָם אַחֵר. יוֹצֵאת
תִּיק עַל גַּבָּהּ, לוּ רַק
הוֹרְתָהּ, אַתֶּם לְכוּ לְחַיֵּיכֶם, הָיֵינוּ

would understand, but she
implores, I am not happy here, let go.

Our hands are stained, we stare at them all morning.
We did not ask for much, exposed to secrets –
in this hollowness to sort out voices, faces,
when hazy light burns over trees, in parlors of
wind, and suicidal rain between the larks in cyber chatter;
It is a sin to thus whet hours into beauty,
to mold from mounting pulse
an entity that precedes it.
No, presence without end, a fleet of wounds
nearing the annulment of all limits.

מְבִינִים אֶת הַדְּבָרִים, אֲבָל הִיא
מַפְּצִירָה, לֹא טוֹב לִי פֹּה, הַרְפּוּ.

יָדֵינוּ עֲקֻבּוֹת, אָנוּ מַבִּיטִים בָּן כָּל הַבֹּקֶר.
מָה כְּבָר בִּקַּשְׁנוּ, מְגִלִּים אֶל רְמָזִים -
בַּחֲלָלוּת הַזֹּאת לָבֹר קוֹלוֹת, פָּנִים
כְּשֶׁאוֹר אָבִיךָ דּוֹלֵק מֵעַל עֵצִים, בִּטְרַקְלִינִים שֶׁל
רוּחַ, וְגֶשֶׁם מִתְאַבֵּד בֵּין עֶפְרוֹנִים בְּסַיְבֶּר הַבַּרְבֶּרֶת;
עָווֹן כָּךְ לְהַשְׁחִיז שָׁעוֹת לְיִפִּי,
לָצוּר מֵהֵלֶם מַחֲרִיף
יֶשְׁנוּת שֶׁהִיא רֵאשִׁית לוֹ.
לֹא, נוֹכְחוּת עַד תֹּם, עַד אֶפֶס גְּבוּלוֹתָיו
מַטָּס שֶׁל שִׁסּוּפִים.

4.

I needed the body as well

to break

but it did not

crash

flocks of birds entered

the flesh

sparrows and bleeding wrens

sap seeping out of balsam trees

frozen as glass, shining

as a plastic scarf

under a moon thrown in the trash

I ceased to see

how I shall live

life anymore

what of

ד.

נִזְקַקְתִּי גַּם לַגּוּף
שֶׁיִּשָּׁבֵר
וְלֹא
נִשְׁבַּר
בָּאוּ סִיעוֹת צִפּוֹרִים
בַּבָּשָׂר
אַנְקוֹרִים חֲשׁוּיִים בְּדָמִים דְּרוֹרִים
שְׂרָף נָטַף מֵעֲצֵי קְטָף
קְפוּאִים כְּמוֹ זְכוּכִית, זוֹרְחִים
כִּרְדִיד נַיְלוֹן
תַּחַת יָרֵחַ מְשֻׁלָּךְ בָּאַשְׁפָּה
חָדַלְתִּי מֵרְאוֹת
אֵיךְ אֶחְיֶה
בַּחַיִּים עוֹד
מִמָּה

5.

And I did not know that I would have to live
your death, and how easily
it would fit into words. Just as mother
explained to the grandchildren, we will
never see Aviva again. And I heard
her cry, not that howling
lamentation, just the flow
of one whose strength vanished in the flame.
And they asked, caught up in wondering,
if you climbed up to a star, what
would you do if it fell, would you be hungry.
And she put them in the bomb
shelter and came sobbing to
the living room where I sat
and said
how simple it is to see
in the dark, like an ember glowing wild—
losing a child means always losing a child.

ה.

וְלֹא יָדַעְתִּי שֶׁאֶצְטָרֵךְ לִחְיוֹת
אֶת מוֹתֵךְ, וְכַמָּה פָּשׁוּט יִהְיֶה לְנַסֵּחַ
אֶת זֶה. כְּמוֹ שֶׁאִמָּא
הִסְבִּירָה לַנְּכָדִים, לֹא נִרְאֶה
אֶת אֲבִיבָה עוֹד אַף פַּעַם. וְשָׁמַעְתִּי
אוֹתָהּ בּוֹכָה, לֹא הַקִּינָה
הַזֹּאת הַמְּנַהֶמֶת, רַק הַשֶּׁטֶף
שֶׁל מִי שֶׁכּוֹחוֹתָיו אָפְסוּ בַּלֶּהָבָה.
וְהֵם שָׁאֲלוּ תְּפוּסֵי תְּמִיהָה
אִם טִפַּסְתִּ לַכּוֹכָב, מָה
תַּעֲשִׂי אִם יִפֹּל, אִם תִּהְיִי רְעֵבָה.
וְהִיא הִנִּיחָה אוֹתָם בְּמִסְתּוֹר
הַקָּסָם וּבָאָה יְפוּחָה אֶל
הַסָּלוֹן שָׁם יָשַׁבְתִּי
וּכְבָר אָמַרְתִּי
כַּמָּה פָּשׁוּט לִרְאוֹת אֶת זֶה
בַּחֲשֵׁכָה כְּמוֹ גַּחֶלֶת -
לְאַבֵּד יֶלֶד פֵּרוּשׁוֹ תָּמִיד לְאַבֵּד יֶלֶד.

6.

She had a heart heavier than the ocean
my mother
and it sank.
Do you feel the desert in your bones?
The sunken ships, stuck
like crosses in the sand, the wells empty
of stars, the pulse of the manna hailing down
do you recall?

1.

הָיָה לָהּ לֵב כָּבֵד מִן הָאוֹקְיָנוֹס
לְאִמִּי
וְהוּא שָׁקַע.
אַתֶּם חָשִׁים בָּעֲצָמוֹת אֶת הַמִּדְבָּר?
אֶת הַסְּפִינוֹת טְבוּעוֹת, תְּקוּעוֹת
בַּחוֹל כְּמוֹ צְלָבִים, אֶת הַבּוֹרוֹת רֵיקִים
מִכּוֹכָבִים, אֶת דֹּפֶק בְּרַד הַמָּן
אַתֶּם זוֹכְרִים?

7.

What were your words
to my sister
in the bathroom, on the
toilet
before
she turned her head to the wall.

Her arms' heft
ripped toilet paper
holder
from its place,
two hand towels
laid out at her feet.

He who sticks His blazing wrath
into mortal affairs,
with Your barren silence, in this morning
of unbearable pain,
You,
tell me—

ז.

מָה הָיָה דִּבָּרְךָ
אֶל אֲחוֹתִי
בַּשֵּׁרוּתִים, עַל
הָאַסְלָה
עַד
שֶׁהֵסַבָּה רֹאשׁ לַקִּיר.

הַכֹּבֶד שֶׁל זְרוֹעָהּ
נִתֵּק מִתְלֵה
נְיַר טוּאָלֶט
מִמְּקוֹמוֹ,
שְׁתֵּי מַגְּבוֹת פָּנִים
יָשְׁרוּ מַרְגְּלוֹתֶיהָ.

הַתּוֹחֵב חֲרוֹן אַפּוֹ
לְעִסְקֵיהֶם שֶׁל בְּנֵי תְּמוּתָה,
בַּשֶּׁקֶט הַמַּחֲרִישׁ שֶׁלְּךָ, בְּבֹקֶר זֶה
שֶׁל חַלְחָלָה,
אֱמֹר לִי גַּם
אַתָּה –

8.

With what else should I praise thee, Lord, when I have praised with a rose's tap, with a cascade of nightingales at dusk, with treetops trimmed by skies of tin, wrought from light, with the lightning's strain dissolving the horizon, on the internet, *Hallel*,
in those hallucinatory depths Your apparition ascends, on the phone's display I praised thee, with a text message: *call me now*,
and I praised thee with my brother's answer, with his city-splitting howl, boring through the ear: You have to come. Aviva, Aviva is dead.

And I praised thee, I praised,
packing my clothes, thrust into lucidity, my legs quivering, *Hallel* at the gates of
the pathology clinic, *Hallel* Abu Kabir, in the oleander hedge I praised,
to its shelter my two brothers and I retreat to fall apart, and with the death certificate
I praised, *Hallel* was always on my lips, driving behind the ambulance
transporting her home, I praised all the way, an unclaimed winter, a clear winter, a winter
bursting bliss, *Hallel* at Nitzanim junction, in the traffic jam I praised, sitting
listening to the thaw's whisper, the ice melting in the container where her body,
autopsy-less, toxic-pure, regathers
its softness.

Thy seraphim
command them to ask
who else has praised thee thus

ח.

בַּמֶּה עוֹד לְהַלְלֶךָ וְהִלַּלְתִּיךָ בִּנְקִישַׁת הַוֶּרֶד, בְּמַפַּל זְמִירִים עִם עֶרֶב, בְּצַמְּרוֹת
בְּדוּלוֹת מִשְּׁמֵי בְּדִיל, קְנוּיוֹת מֵאוֹר, בְּמֶתַח הַבָּרָק
הַמְּפָרֵק בָּאֹפֶק, עַל בָּמוֹת הָאִינְטֶרְנֶט הַלֵּל בַּמַּעֲמַקִּים
הַהֲזוּיִים אַתָּה מוֹפִיעַ כְּרָפָא, בְּצַג הַסִּלוּלָרִי
הִלַּלְתִּיךָ, בְּהוֹדָעַת הַטֶּקְסְט: תְּקַשֵּׁר דָּחוּף,
וְהִלַּלְתִּיךָ בִּתְשׁוּבַת אָחִי, בְּהֶמְיָתוֹ חוֹתֶכֶת הֶעָרִים, רוֹצַעַת אֶת הָאֹזֶן:
אַתָּה חַיָּב לָבוֹא, אֲבִיבָה, אֲבִיבָה מֵתָה.

וְהִלַּלְתִּיךָ, הִלַּלְתִּיךָ,
אוֹרֵז אֶת הַבְּגָדִים, נֶחְבָּט אֶל הַצְּלִילוֹת, רַגְלַי מָטוֹת, הַלֵּל בְּשַׁעֲרֵי
הַפָּתוֹלוֹגְיָה, הַלֵּל אַבּוּ כַּבִּיר, בִּמְשׁוּכוֹת הַרְדּוּף הִלַּלְתִּי,
אֶל מִסְתּוֹרָן אֲנִי וּשְׁנֵי אַחַי חוֹמְקִים לְהִשָּׁבֵר, וּבִתְעוּדַת פְּטִירָה
הִלַּלְתִּי, לֹא מָשׁ מִבֵּין שְׂפָתַי הַלֵּל, נוֹסְעִים מֵאֲחוֹרֵי הָאַמְבּוּלַנְס
הַמּוֹבִילָה הַבַּיְתָה, הִלַּלְתִּי כָּל הַדֶּרֶךְ, חֹרֶף מִפְּרָז, חֹרֶף נָקִי, חֹרֶף שִׁטּוּף
עֶדְנָה, הַלֵּל בְּצֹמֶת נִצָּנִים, בִּפְקַק תְּנוּעָה הִלַּלְתִּי, יוֹשְׁבִים
מַאֲזִינִים לְרַחַשׁ הַפִּשָּׁרָה, הַקֶּרַח הַנָּמֵס בַּמְּכוּלָה בָּהּ גּוּפָתָהּ
דְּחוּיַת הַנְּתִיחָה, הַטְּהוֹרָה מֵרַעַל, אוֹסֶפֶת שׁוּב
אֶת רַכּוּתָהּ.

שְׂרָפֶיךָ
צַו וְיִשָּׁאֲלוּ
מִי הִלַּלְךָ עוֹד כֹּה מֵעַל

over the tar's timbre, through the asphalt's roar, in an air of slackened honey,
and who had exalted your name with a sister, with her fleeting breath in the bathroom, with a conquered heart and with flesh lying on the floor, turning blue,
bursting with a splendor of eternal silence, with a mother desperately kissing it
Who had once lauded thee.

זִמְרַת הַזֶּפֶת, מֵעֵבֶר דְּכִי אַסְפַּלְט, בִּדְבַשׁ רָפוּי שֶׁל הָאַוִיר,
וּמִי קִדֵּשׁ שִׁמְךָ בַּאֲחוֹתוֹ, בִּנְשִׁימָתָהּ הַחַטּוּפָה בְּבֵית שִׁמּוּשׁ, בְּלֵב
כָּבוּשׁ וּבְבָשָׂר שׁוֹכֵב עַל הָרִצְפָּה, מַכְחִיל,
נִמְלָא הַדְרַת דּוּמָה, בָּאֵם הַמְכַסָּה אוֹתוֹ בִּנְשִׁיקוֹת
מִי קִלַּסְךָ.

9.

At the dawn of *Kislev*
she suddenly knew
the will of the body is the source of the Fall,
not like then, in that ancient story
of knowledge, of flesh, or maybe it's always been
thus—a plea to exceed, to shatter the limit,
only thus will it be met, reaching an other.
How will it reach, if in order to pass it is forced
to cancel its stay. It is slaughtered towards the desire for space,
towards its error of middle-grounds, which thus turn concrete,
which require a linkage that, through affinity, can call out with strength:
get to know us, oh body, and we will be for you.
But she, she knew well, the thing that appears
at the end of the night like a light is
her gate, when darkness is rolled up away
from the world—what does it mean to follow the will of the body;
she had the choice to leave,
to shed off the cold-snaps of the year,
leaving the garden withered and sere,
almond calyxes trapped in follicles, a purple blossom
within the corolla, to undo in her room explosives of chance,
the crestfallen ending of an O. Henry tale,

ט.

בְּשַׁחַר כִּסְלֵו לְפֶתַע יָדֶעָה
רְצוֹן הַגּוּף הוּא יוֹצֵר הַגְּרוּשׁ,
לֹא כְּמוֹ אָז, בַּסִּפּוּר הַיָּשָׁן
עַל יֶדַע, בָּשָׂר, וְאוּלַי מִתָּמִיד זֶה
הָיָה – תְּחִנָּה לַחֹרֹג, לְשַׁבֵּר אֶת הַגְּבוּל,
שֶׁרַק כָּךְ הוּא יֻשְׁלַם, כְּשֶׁיֵּצֵא אֶל אַחֵר.
אֵיךְ יֵצֵא, אִם כְּדֵי לַעֲבֹר הוּא מֻדָּח
אֶל בִּטּוּל הַשְּׁהוּת. הוּא נִטְבָּח אֶל תְּשׁוּקַת הַמִּרְוָח,
אֶל טָעוּת שְׁרִיָּתוֹ בַּבֵּינַיִם, הַהוֹפְכִים לְמַמָּשׁ, הַזְּקוּקִים לַזְּקָה,
רַק הַיַּחַס נוֹתֵן לָהֶם כּוֹחַ לִקְרֹא:
הַכִּירֵנוּ, הוֹ, גּוּף, וְנִהְיֶה בִּשְׁבִילְךָ.
אֲבָל הִיא, הִיא יָדֶעָה, הַדָּבָר הֶעָשׂוּי
בְּתֻמּוֹ שֶׁל לַיְלָה כְּמוֹ אוֹר הוּא
הַשַּׁעַר שֶׁלָּהּ, בִּגְלִילַת הַחֹשֶׁךְ מִפְּנֵי
הָעוֹלָם – מָה פֵּשֶׁר מִלּוּי רְצוֹנוֹ שֶׁל הַגּוּף:
רְשׁוּתָהּ זוֹ הָיְתָה לַעֲזֹב,
לְהַשִּׁיל מֵעַצְמָהּ אֶת קָרוֹת הַשָּׁנָה
הָעוֹמְדוֹת לוֹחֲצוֹת אֶת צְמִיחַת הַגִּנָּה,
גְּבִיעֵי שָׂקֵד בְּתוֹךְ זְקִיקֵיהֶם, תִּפְרַחַת סְגֻלָּה
בְּתוֹךְ כּוֹתָרוֹת, לִפְרֹק בְּחַדְרָהּ חֲזִיזִים שֶׁל אַקְרַאי
סוֹפוֹ הֶעָגוּם שֶׁל סִפּוּר שֶׁל אוֹ הֶנְרִי,
קַנָּאוּת שֶׁל ז׳וּל וֶרְן לִפְרָטֵי הַמַּפּוֹת, צִטּוּט

Jules Verne's acuteness to a fine map's detail, a quote
by Miss Lamb or her husband,
Shakespeare flayed of poetry.
Yes, her permission it was, and thus it shall stay,
because we were plunged into no lesser a chore: to measure
her distance with a heart full of grime, to write down
her movement stripped bare of time—

שֶׁל הַגְּבֶרֶת לֶמֶב אוֹ שֶׁל בַּעֲלָהּ,
שֶׁקִּסְפִּיר פָּשׁוּט מֵעוֹר הַשִּׁירָה.
כֵּן, רְשׁוּתָהּ זוֹ הָיְתָה, וּרְשׁוּתָהּ זוֹ תִּהְיֶה,
כִּי אָנוּ הוּטַלְנוּ לִשְׁהוּת לֹא פְּחוּתָה: חִשּׁוּב
מֶרְחַקֶּיהָ בְּלֵב מְלֵבָן, רִשּׁוּם
תְּנוּעָתָהּ הַנִּקִּית מִן הַזְּמַן -

10.

The residents discovered the bougainvillea: slender necks, quivering
lips. Calyces
hammered hammered
with tough brightness. The colors
lost their names in showers of sunlight,
in *Tevethian* shards of frost.
Yitgadales and *Yitkadashes*
stole across the garden's end.

ו.

הַתּוֹשָׁבִים גִּלּוּ אֶת הַבּוּגֶנְוִילְיָה: צַוָּארִים דַּקִּים, שְׂפָתַיִם
רוֹטְטוֹת. גְּבִיעִים
רְקוּעִים רְקוּעִים
נְהָרָה קְשׁוּחָה. הַצְּבָעִים
אִבְּדוּ אֶת שְׁמָם בְּקִלּוּחֵי שֶׁמֶשׁ
בִּמְכִתּוֹת כְּפוֹר מְטֻבָּתוֹת.
צְלוֹת וּבָעוּת
גָּנְבוּ אֶת גְּבוּל הַגִּנָּה.

11.

Salvation and fear turned into thorns—
a bird shrieked in the olive tree thicket;
a bird chiseled sound in the rain.
My body succumbed to the inheritance, pulsing: possibilities
of pain, the spilt quiddity
of the blood, whole—
heartedness demanded by others.

יא.

יְשׁוּעָה וּפַחַד הָיוּ לִצְנִינִים –
צִפּוֹר צָלְלָה בִּסְבַךְ עֵץ הַזַּיִת;
צִפּוֹר חָרְצָה קוֹל בַּגֶּשֶׁם.
גּוּפִי נַעֲנָה לַיְרֻשָּׁה בְּהֹלֶם: אֶפְשָׁרוּיוֹת
שֶׁל כְּאֵב, עַצְמוּתוֹ הַשְּׁפוּכָה
שֶׁל הַדָּם, חֵפֶץ –
לֵב שֶׁטָּבְעוּ אֲחֵרִים.

12.

Shevat crept in coils of ice, cracks
of expanding control, a constant zeppelin flickered,
let drop from a god's mind. To give in to it—to capture the predictable
in crystal spheres carrying stars, to register
the bearings' mechanical moans as the nights shift,
a translucent halo rising like vapor from beyond the growth
and its ebbing strength, veil
over veil, sheets of light exposed by their unease, a divination
in larks and strips of clouds—
there is a structure, a design, or at least a demand for
man to bow his head, to slice paths
in the air, to rise above his life
to some height, be as a poet, believing
he will catch in paintings
something of human sorrow. No, not
what you've wanted,
metaphysics is the origin of havoc. To betray
this then—roam the world
as angels deaf to Aramaic,
striving for existence in the body,
to learn how to subside in a *Shevat*
furrowed with frost. The wild carrot is all conceit, its sole purpose

יב.

טִפֵּס שֶׁבֶט בִּקְנוֹקָנוֹת שֶׁל קֶרַח, סְדָקִים
שֶׁל הַרְחָבַת שִׁלְטוֹן, צֶפֶלִין־תָּמִיד הִבְהֵב,
שָׁמוּט מִזִּכְרוֹנוֹ שֶׁל אֵל. לְהִתְמַסֵּר לָזֶה – לִתְפֹּס אֶת הַצָּפוּי
בְּגַלְגַּלֵּי הַבְּרֹלַח נוֹשְׂאֵי הַכּוֹכָבִים, לִרְשֹׁם
אֶת יִבֵּבַת הַמְּסַבִּים כְּשֶׁהַלֵּילוֹת נָעִים,
הִלָּה שְׁקוּפָה עוֹלָה כְּאֵד מֵעֵבֶר לַצְּמִיחָה
וְכוֹחוֹתֶיהָ הַכָּלִים, צָעִיף
וְעוֹד צָעִיף, אֶת יְרִיעוֹת הָאוֹר תַּסְגִּיר עַצְבָּנוּתָן, נִחוּשׁ
בְּעֶפְרוֹנִים וּרְצוּעוֹת עָנָן –
מַתְכֹּנֶת יֵשׁ, אַדְרִיכָלוּת, אוֹ לְפָחוֹת תְּבִיעָה מִן
הָאָדָם לָשֹׂחַ אֶת רֹאשׁוֹ, לִבְצֹעַ בָּאֲוִיר
שְׁבִילִים, לְהִתְרוֹמֵם מֵעִם חַיָּיו
אֶל אֵיזֶה גֹּבַהּ, לִהְיוֹת כַּמְּשׂוֹרֵר, סָבוּר
שֶׁיִּתְבּוֹנֵן בְּצִיּוּרִים
אֶל תּוֹךְ דָּבָר שֶׁל יִסּוּרֵי אֱנוֹשׁ. לֹא, לֹא
מָה שֶׁרָצִית,
הַמֵּטָפִיזִיקָה תְּהֵא רֵאשִׁית הַחִדָּלוֹן. לִבְגֹּד
בָּזֶה אִם כֵּן – כְּמַלְאָכִים אֲשֶׁר חֵרְשִׁים
לָאֲרָמִית לָלֶכֶת בָּעוֹלָם,
חוֹתְרִים אֶל מַמָּשׁוּת בַּגּוּף,
לִלְמֹד לְהִצְטַמְצֵם בִּשְׁבָט חָרוּשׁ
הַכְּפוֹר. גֶּזֶר הַגִּנָּה הוּא רַק גָּאוֹן שֶׁתַּכְלִיתוֹ

is to bend under the burden of the self, the rose— whirlpool of color, a rustle
fit for fragrancy.
No, not that? What was the flower you desired? The *sheizava*?
Here it is, as you have wished, clear as alcohol,
the effort of its foliage brought a bloody sun above it. And it is ripe—
reach out your hand.

כְּרִיעָה תַּחַת עֵלוֹ שֶׁל הָעַצְמִי, הַוֶּרֶד – מְעַרְבֹּלֶת צֶבַע, אִוּוּשׁ יָפֶה לַבְּשָׂמִים.

לֹא, לֹא זֶה? מָה הַפֶּרַח שֶׁבְּקַשְׁתְּ? הַשֵּׁיזָבָא?

הִנֵּה הִיא כִּרְעוּתֵךְ צְלוּלָה כְּאַלְכּוֹהוֹל,

בְּטֹרַח עַלְוָתָהּ זְרֻחָה עָלֶיהָ שֶׁמֶשׁ דָּם. וְזוֹהִי עוֹנָתָהּ -

הוֹשִׁיטִי אֶת יָדֵךְ.

13.

The sun—an old man falls asleep in the sun; the light,
soured milk,
entifies objects. All animals
can endure the endless. But
finitude. In my sleep I do not cease
to hear: lowing, a short sharp
howl, the windy
flicker of the rose's
flame, that quivering
quiver.

יג.

הַשֶּׁמֶשׁ – זָקֵן נִרְדָּם בַּשֶּׁמֶשׁ; חָלָב
שֶׁהֶחְמִיץ הָאוֹר
מִיַּשִּׁישׁ עַצְמִים. כָּל חַיָּה
בְּכוֹחָהּ לָשֵׂאת אֵינְסוֹף. אֲבָל
הַסּוֹף. בִּשְׁנָתִי לֹא אֶחְדַּל
לִשְׁמֹעַ: גְּעִיָּה, יְלָלָה
דַּקַּת דֶּקֶר, הָזַע
הָרוּחַ אֶת לַהַט
הַוֶּרֶד, הָרַעַד הַהוּא
הָרוֹעֵד.

14.

Where are you? Under a pillow I laid a book
you gave me
my first book
your inscription inside—handwriting clear as
a cut.
My dreams were an empty temple. I waited and waited till
morning.

יד.

הֵיכָן אַתְּ? תַּחַת כַּר הִנַּחְתִּי סֵפֶר
שֶׁנָּתַתְּ לִי
הַסֵּפֶר הָרִאשׁוֹן שֶׁלִּי
הַקְּדָשָׁתֵךְ בַּפֶּתַח – כְּתַב־יָד נָקִי כְּמוֹ
חֶתֶךְ.
הָיוּ חֲלוֹמוֹתַי הֵיכָל רֵיק. חִכִּיתִי וְחִכִּיתִי עַד
הַבֹּקֶר.

Clangs on the anvil of light
that will eventually bisect me
since my birth I hear with woe

Word by word my body is sung
dares dangerously to enter
with my own eyes to know.

(Poetry, 2)

הַלְמוּת חִשּׁוּל הָאוֹר
שֶׁיְּבַתְּרֵנִי לְבַסּוֹף
מִלֵּדָתִי אֲנִי שׁוֹמֵעַ

מִלָּה מִלָּה גּוּפִי מוּשָׁר
הוֹרֵס אֵלָיו לָבוֹא
בְּמוֹ עֵינַי לְהִתְוַדֵּעַ.

(שִׁירָה, 2)

15.

Let me have those shapes that shrivel language
And I shall break them up limb by limb,
I shall lay bare their roots,
their evil-doings I shall dash against the stone,
malicious sluts say Aviva is gone.
But I was
as well, Hebrew pounding on
my throat-bell, I answered aye.
It has the dick of a camel, that one.

טו.

הָבוּ לִי אֶת הַצּוּרוֹת הַמְּצֻרוֹת אֶת הַשָּׂפָה
וַאֲפַרְקֵן אֵיבָר־אֵיבָר,
אֶעֱרֹן עַד הַיְסוֹד, מַעֲלָלָן
אֶשְׁבֹּר אֶל סֶלַע,
שַׁרְמוּטוֹת אֲיֻמּוֹת אוֹמְרוֹת אֲבִיבָה מֵתָה.
אֲבָל הָיִיתִי גַּם
אֲנִי, דָּפְקָה עִבְרִית בְּתוֹךְ
גְּרוֹנִי, עָנִיתִי הֵן.
זֹאת זַיִן שֶׁל גָּמָל יֵשׁ לָהּ.

16.

What is wrong with them, the mustard plants, that they are irritated thus all of a sudden,
bellflowers nearing pungency under the oppression of midday
the marigold, it too is burning molecules of oxygen, arising
in their presence like the chariot's celestial wheels.
What season is it now, I do not wish to say: clusters of computers
have yet to flicker information like neurons in a network, skies have
yet to be produced in sweatshops, viewers dumbfounded before them,
letting drop from their mind the children going blind in the process of their welding,
hammers frozen in midair. Is that their noise, coming from outside?
Perhaps it's winter, seems like winter, thunders then, surely
not a sigh
of someone knocking on a door, with no reply,
and the mother then awakens, the door withdrawing in answer to her touch,
she sees – the daughter sitting
dressed in rags of dawn, ready for the journey,
she calls her name, then screams, spraying her with perfume,
the daughter opens up an eye, then lets go. It's done, her voice breaks down, she's gone.
We're now alone, dispatched instead of
I-loved-you-so, a-brother's-duty,
breathing purified air
and the fallow land around flows unblemished—
What is wrong with them, the warblers, that they whisper thus,

טז.

מָה יֵשׁ לָהֶם לַחַרְדָּלִים שֶׁכָּךְ הֵם נִרְגָּזִים פִּתְאוֹם,
עֲנִבָּלִים עַזִּים כִּמְעַט בְּלַחַץ צָהֳרַיִם
צִפֹּרֶן הֶחָתוּל גַּם לָהּ שְׁרֵפַת מוֹלֵקוּלוֹת חַמְצָן, עוֹלָה
לְעָמָתָם כָּאֲפָנִים.
מָה הָעוֹנָה, אֵינִי חָפֵץ לוֹמַר: עוֹד לֹא הֶצְבּוּ צְבִירֵי
מַחְשֵׁב מְהַבְהֲבִים מֵידָע כִּרְשָׁתוֹת נוֹירוֹנִים, עוֹד לֹא הוּצְאוּ שְׁחָקִים
מִסַּדְנְאוֹת הַיַּזַּע, וְנֶעֱמְדוּ הַמִּשְׁתָּאִים מוּלָם,
שׁוֹמְטִים מִזִּכְרוֹנָם אֶת הַיְלָדִים הַמְּאַבְּדִים רֵאוֹת בְּחִשּׁוּלָם,
וּמַקָּבוֹת קְפוּאוֹת בְּהֶגְפָּן. זֶה רַעֲשָׁן, הָרְעָשִׁים מִתּוֹךְ הַחוּץ?
אוּלַי בְּעֶצֶם חֹרֶף, נִדְמֶה שֶׁחֹרֶף, וּרְעָמִים אֵפוֹא, וַדַּאי
לֹא נְקִישָׁה
שֶׁל אִישׁ נוֹקֵשׁ עַל דֶּלֶת, לֹא נַעֲנֶה,
וּמִקִּיצָה הָאֵם, לְמַגָּעָהּ הַדֶּלֶת נְסוֹגָה, רוֹאָה – הַבַּת יוֹשֶׁבֶת
לְבוּשָׁה בִּבְלוֹא שֶׁל שַׁחַר, דְּרוּכָה אֶל הַמַּסָּע,
קוֹרֵאת בִּשְׁמָהּ, אַחַר כָּךְ הִיא צוֹעֶקֶת, בִּשֵּׁם הִיא מַזָּה,
הַבַּת פּוֹקַחַת עַיִן, סוֹגֶרֶתָּהּ. זֶהוּ זֶה, נִשְׁבָּר קוֹלָהּ, הָלְכָה.
אֲנַחְנוּ נִשָּׁאֵר, מְשֻׁלָּחִים בִּמְקוֹם
אַהֲבָתִי־כָּל־כָּךְ, כְּפִי־חוֹבָתִי־כֹּאַח,
נוֹשְׁמִים אֲוִיר צָרוּף
וּמֶרְחֲבֵי הַבּוּר סָבִיב זוֹרְמִים בְּטֹהַר---
מָה יֵשׁ לָהֶם לַפָּשׁוֹשִׁים שֶׁכָּךְ הֵם רוֹחֲשִׁים,
מֵחִכּוּכָם גִּצִּים נוֹרִים, זֶה זָהֳרָם, הַזֹּהַר הַמֵּמִיס אֶת הַגְּבוּלוֹת?

from their friction sparks flare out, is that their radiance that melts down all the borders?
Spring fades into summer, gold eddies
on the leaves, not that gold of rings slipped off
from a daughter's dead fingers, not that necklace
bursting bright in the shop windows of London, somewhere close
to Baker street. A bright cargo,
time-of-then bridled in gold:
I am not sixteen enough, the moment of goodbye
was not yet desecrated, you will not yet give words of advice,
not yet command, remember:
to write you must trace
the halting place of your heart,
nearing there backwards
is poetry's art.

אָבִיב נָמוֹג אֶל קַיִץ, זָהָב הַמְּפַכְּפֵךְ
עַל הֶעָלִים, לֹא זְהַב הַטַּבָּעוֹת הַמְּשֻׁלּוֹת
מֵאֶצְבָּעוֹת מֵתוֹת שֶׁל בַּת, לֹא הָרָבִיד
הַמִּתְפָּרֵץ בָּרָק בְּחַלּוֹנוֹת הָרַאֲוָה שֶׁל לוֹנְדוֹן, הֵיכַנְשֶׁהוּ סָמוּךְ
לְבֵיקֶר סְטְרִיט. זָהָב,
מִטְעָן בָּהִיר, זְמַן־אָז אָסוּר בְּפָז:
אֵינִי מַסְפִּיק בֶּן שֵׁשׁ־עֶשְׂרֵה, הָרֵגַע לַפְּרִדָה
עוֹד לֹא חָלַל, עוֹד לֹא תִּתְּנִי עֵצָה לַדֶּרֶךְ,
וְלֹא תּוֹרִי זָכוֹר,
כְּדֵי לִכְתֹּב אַתֵּר
הֵיכָן לִבְּךָ עוֹמֵד,
הַהִתְקָרְבוּת הַלֹּא נִגְמֶרֶת חֲזָרָה
זוֹ הַשִּׁירָה.

17.

And I once already learned
to live off poetry.
I labored to discern
the chrysanthemums' haste
from seared angels
crucified on stems,
swallows boasting on air
from crumbs of coal.
I knew which would be harder,
the Fall
down from bliss
up from Terra—

יז.

וּפַעַם כְּבָר לָמַדְתִּי
לִחְיוֹת מִן הַשִּׁירָה.
שֶׁכְּלַלְתִּי לְהַבְדִּיל
פַּחַז חַרְצִיּוֹת מִמַּלְאָכִים צְרוּבִים
צְלוּבִים עַל גִּבְעוֹלִים,
סִיסֵי חוֹמוֹת מִתְפָּאֲרִים עַל הָאֲוִיר
מֵחֲתִיכוֹת פֶּחָם.
יָדַעְתִּי מָה קָשָׁה יוֹתֵר
הַנְּפִילָה
מַטָּה מֵעֶדְנָה
מַעְלָה מֵאַרְעָא -

18.

But if compelled to give form to
my sister— and if I ask someone
to name a force of nature,
surely then a word
will be replaced with
a reply, a desire
to be a construct, a contradiction,
and I'll be answered, always answered thus:
a pillar of storm or the heavy heat of *Tammuz* or
the lily's sepal breaking through a bed of *Kurkar* sand—
how will I, then, how will I speak
her.

יח.

אַךְ אִם אֲנִי אָנוּס לָתֵת דְּמוּת
לַאֲחוֹתִי – וְאִם אֶשְׁאַל אֵי מִי
לוֹמַר לִי כּוֹחַ טֶבַע מָה
הֲלוֹא אָז תִּתְחַלֵּף מִלָּה
בְּפִתְרוֹן, תְּשׁוּקָה
לִהְיוֹת בִּנְיָן, סְתִירָה,
וְאֵעָנֶה, תָּמִיד כָּךְ נַעֲנֶה:
עַמּוּד סוּפָה אוֹ שְׁרַב תַּמּוּז אוֹ
גְּבִיעַ חֲבַצֶּלֶת שׁוֹבֵר מַצַּע כְּרְכָּר –
כֵּיצַד אֲנִי, אִם כֵּן, אֵיךְ אֲדַבֵּר
אוֹתָהּ.

19.

One can sing of rain, the mightiness
of water, all through the shiv'ah corpulent clouds
rubbed against the softness
of the mourners' tent, and of the slightest of them one can sing,
now on the dawn of *Shevat*,
infidel frost over the greyish lawn, there your childhood,
and there your fallen life is crammed:

Your locks are full of shards
after a shower, through which you've run your fingers
and did not brush, even when they chided, a smile on your lips,
you read Austen, that British bitch has
a sharp wit, as fog dwellers usually do, outline of geography,

and a teacher's comments of amazement, reddish
upon the copied desert maps, distances
you've crossed, fixed within Sderot, asphalt lines
reaching your students, disquieting problems
of geometry.

Could you have guessed all this was
before you came to know it,

יט.

אֶפְשָׁר לָשִׁיר עַל גְּשָׁמִים, גְּבוּרוֹת
הַמַּיִם, כָּל הַשִּׁבְעָה כִּרְסֵי הָעֲנָנִים
חֻכְּכוּ בְּרֹךְ חִפַּת
הָאֲבֵלִים, וְעַל הַדַּק מֵהֶם אֶפְשָׁר לָשִׁיר,
עַכְשָׁו בְּשַׁחַר שְׁבָט,
כָּפֵר עַל דֶּשֶׁא אֲפַרְפַּר, שָׁם יַלְדוּתֵךְ,
וְשָׁם חַיַּיִךְ הַמֵּתִים דְּחוּקִים:

קְוֻצּוֹתַיִךְ מְלֵאוֹת שְׁבָרִים
מִן הַמִּקְלַחַת, שֶׁהֶעֱבַרְתְּ בָּן אֶת יָדֵךְ
וְלֹא סֵרַקְתְּ, גַּם כְּשֶׁהֵעִירוּ, חִיּוּךְ עַל שִׂפְתוֹתַיִךְ,
קָרֵאת בְּאוֹסְטֶן, חוּשׁ הוּמוֹר מֻשְׁחָז יֵשׁ
לַכַּלְבָּה הַבְּרִיטִית, בִּכְלָל לָהֶם יוֹשְׁבֵי הָעֲרָפֶל, סִכּוּם בְּגֵאוֹגְרַפְיָה,

וְסִמּוּנֵי הַהִשְׁתָּאוּת שֶׁל הַמּוֹרָה, אַדְמוּמִיִּים עַל
הַמַּפּוֹת הַמְּעֻתָּקוֹת שֶׁל הַמִּדְבָּר, מֶרְחַקִּים
שֶׁאַתְּ צָלַחְתְּ, קְבוּעִים בְּתוֹךְ שְׁדֵרוֹת, קַוֵּי אַסְפַלְט
מִמֵּךְ אֶל תַּלְמִידַיִךְ, סֻגִּיּוֹת עוֹכְרוֹת שַׁלְוָה
בְּגֵאוֹמֶטְרִיָּה.

הַאִם שִׁעַרְתְּ שֶׁכָּל זֶה כְּבָר הָיָה
בְּטֶרֶם הִתְוַדַּעְתְּ לוֹ,

because the future has occurred and it's blowing
your way you
who are time resistant—

The end of time has wakened, will
you not hear, in the air's fortress,
among the dewdrops, the almond tree quivers at its blossoms, no,
it has quivered,

no, the planted trees have dried out, the growing flora have expired, the earth has vomited
its heart, and it's enormous,
breathing your breath, light had descended like iron,
so refined, filled its space below
the whole world has broken so, facing Aviva-no.

כִּי הֶעָתִיד אֵרַע וְהוּא נוֹשֵׁב
אֵלַיִךְ אַתְּ
הָעֲמִידָה לַזְּמַן –

קֵץ הַיָּמִים הֵקִיץ, הַאִם
לֹא תִּשְׁמְעִי, בְּתוֹךְ מִבְצַר הָאֲוִירִים,
בֵּין הַטְּלָלִים, הַשְּׁקֵדִיָּה נִרְעֶדֶת מִפְּרִיחָה, לֹא,
הִיא נִרְעֶדָה,

לֹא, הָעֵצִים הַנִּטָּעִים יָבֵשׁוּ, כָּלְתָה הַצִּמְחִיָּה אֲשֶׁר תִּצְמַח, הָאֲדָמָה הֵקִיאָה
אֶת לִבָּהּ, וְהוּא עֲנָק
נוֹשֵׁם אֶת נִשְׁמָתֵךְ, הָאוֹר יָרַד כְּבַרְזְלִים,
הָדוּר כָּל כָּךְ, מָלֵא אֶת חֲלָלוֹ
הָעוֹלָם הֻכְרַע כֻּלּוֹ אֶל מוּל אֲבִיבָהּ־לֹא.

20.

A stretched glimmer is the glass
on the window, bliss it was
deserted in that grove.

I took a stone—
a piece
she scorched for me
said I should look
through it at the sun.

It was a eucalyptus grove,
its scent awakened, waned.
Its flames idle, rustling,
green glint burst
from them, drowned

in a light hard with soot,
a little cloud. Thirty
years my back was turned to
her moment of escape

כ.

נִיצוֹץ מָתוּחַ הַזִּכּוּכִית
עַל פְּנֵי הַחַלּוֹן, חֶמְדָּה הָיְתָה
בְּחֹרֶשׁ עֲזוּבָה.

אֲנִי לָקַחְתִּי אֶבֶן, הִיא –
פִּסָּה
חָרְכָה לְמַעֲנִי
אָמְרָה לִי לְהַבִּיט
בַּשֶּׁמֶשׁ בַּעֲדָהּ.

הָיָה חֹרֶשׁ אֵיקָלִיפְּטוּס,
רֵיחוֹ הֵקִיץ, כָּבָה.
לְהָבָיו נִרְפִּים, מְאֻוָּשִׁים,
בָּרָק יָרֹק זִגֵּק גָּמִישׁ
מֵהֶם, טָבַע

בְּאוֹר נָחוּשׁ בְּפִיחַ,
עֲנָנָה, שְׁלוֹשִׁים
שָׁנָה גַּבִּי הוּסַב אֶל
זְמַן חֲמִיקָתָהּ

towards what, towards some truth:

In these reins—
love—
lies the utter power to release us from ourselves
but so they also mean
to place in another's hands
the right to make us lonely.

לְעֵבֶר מָה, לְאֵיזוֹ יְדִיעָה:

בַּמּוֹסֵרוֹת הָאֵלֶּה -
אַהֲבָה -
הַכּוֹחַ הַגָּמוּר לְהַתִּירֵנוּ מֵעַצְמֵנוּ
מִשּׁוּם כָּךְ גַּם פֵּרוּשָׁן
לָתֵת בִּידֵי אַחֵר רְשׁוּת
לַעֲשׂוֹתֵנוּ בּוֹדְדִים.

21.

The body knew what it knew
and kept silent.

Trees spoke. The sun spoke
with heightened
courage. Night divided
into shifts of poetry.

The wind swept away the murmur,
God's stars eroded like
bones.

And she smiled, withdrew from the moon held
between the thumb and the forefinger, its light
diluted in the television's glow. She smiled,
Men achieved all that, American footsteps in space,
prints of dust and time.

She smiled, knitting patterns into
yarmulkes with one needle. She smiled when sketching
them on graphing paper, in those cages of squares,
smiled when her girls came

כא.

הַגּוּף יָדַע מָה שֶׁיָּדַע
וְהֶחֱרִישׁ.

עֵצִים דִּבְּרוּ. דִּבֵּר הַשֶּׁמֶשׁ
בִּגְבוּרָה
גְּבוֹהָה. לַיְלָה נֶחְלַק
לְמִשְׁמְרוֹת שִׁירָה.

הָרוּחַ טִאְטְאָה אֶת הַמִּלְמוּל,
כּוֹכְבֵי יָהּ שְׁחוּקִים כְּמוֹ
עֲצָמוֹת.

וְהִיא חִיְּכָה, מִן הַיָּרֵחַ נָסוֹגָה, אָחוּז
בֵּין אֲגוּדָל וְאֶצְבַּע, אוֹרוֹ
נִמְהָל בְּאוֹר הַטֵּלֵוִיזְיָה. חִיְּכָה,
יַד אָדָם הִשִּׁיגָה אֶת כָּל זֶה, סִלְיוֹת חָלָל אָמֵרִיקָאִיּוֹת,
טְבִיעוֹת אָבָק וּזְמַן.

חִיְּכָה, סוֹרֶגֶת דִּגְמָאוֹת לְתוֹךְ
כִּפּוֹת בְּמַסְרֵגָה אַחַת. חִיְּכָה גַּם כְּשֶׁתִּכְּנָה
אוֹתָן בְּמַחְבְּרוֹת חֶשְׁבּוֹן, בִּכְלוּב הַמִּשְׁבְּצוֹת,
חִיְּכָה כְּשֶׁבָּאוּ תַּלְמִידוֹת מִן הַכִּתָּה

tortured in starched blouses, in their burning virginity, copying
notes: forms and languages. She smiled, for years she has
been leaving
things to their images.

Attila lashed into the wilderness like a whip, like dawn, like
birds, the Greeks and their logic, their palpable
passion, Assyria cut through with razors of fire,
these were all fluctuations on an axis,
a flowchart.

Then she went
to Tel Aviv by bus. An enthused young man
apprised her of the
information age—pinheads,
digits compressed in nonspace,
the speed of light.

She returned. It was waiting, that same house, where her mother
brought her forth. It expected her, the room,
ready to receive her own *tzimtzum*. And she
smiled, it was

סְגוּפוֹת בְּסַד חֻלְצָה, בִּבְתוּלֵיהֶן הַבּוֹעֲרִים, הֶעֱתִיקוּ
סִכּוּמִים: מִבְנִים וּלְשׁוֹנוֹת. חִיכָּה, שָׁנִים שֶׁהִיא
הִנִּיחָה
אֶת הַדְּבָרִים לִדְמוּמָם.

אָטִילָה הַמְּצִלָּף בָּעֲרָבוֹת כְּמוֹ שׁוֹט, כְּמוֹ שַׁחַר, כְּמוֹ
צִפּוֹר, הַיְּוָנִים וְהֶגְיוֹנָם, תְּשׁוּקָתָם הַמּוּחָשִׁית
כָּל כָּךְ, אַשּׁוּר הַחֲתוּכָה בְּתַעַר אֵשׁ,
כֻּלָּם הָיוּ תְּנוּדָה עַל צִיר,
תַּרְשִׁים זְרִימָה.

אַחַר כָּךְ גַּם נָסְעָה
בָּאוֹטוֹבּוּס לְתֵל אָבִיב. בָּחוּר נִרְגָּשׁ
בִּשֵּׁר לָהּ עַל רֵאשִׁית
עִדַּן הָאִינְפּוֹרְמַצְיָה – רָאשֵׁי סִכָּה,
סְפָרוֹת דְּחוּסוֹת בְּאֵינְחָלָל,
מְהִירוּת אוֹר.

חָזְרָה. הִמְתִּין אוֹתוֹ הַבַּיִת, שָׁם חִבְּלָתָה
אִמָּהּ. חִכָּה הַחֶדֶר
נָכוֹן לִקְלֹט אֶת צִמְצוּמָהּ. וְהִיא
חִיכָּה, הָיָה

raining outside the window, thundered air, the mistake has just been known

Men

were sure

that history

had a purpose of its own.

גָּשׁוּם מֵעֵבֶר לַחַלּוֹן, אֲוִיר רָעוּם, הַטָּעוּת זֶה הֶשְׁלְמָה
בְּנֵי אָדָם
הָיוּ בְּטוּחִים
שֶׁלַּהִיסְטוֹרְיָה
יֵשׁ תַּכְלִית בִּפְנֵי
עַצְמָהּ.

22.

I recall the flame tree made taut with summer
in Sderot,
its reddish dawn is also
a Strip of fire.

Nothing's scorched, skin
nor sight: it's here we came, my sweaty
palm clawed
in yours.

And here you set me down, showed me
the books. A braid you had,
there were your eyes, you did not know
how redeemed
you were already.

Thirteen years old, delivered from
the flesh, breathing air whose
nature is unknown. And the world
trembled, the world raged, thrusts of light
like chariots. You grasped
the movement, the dismemberment, you raised

כב.

זָכַרְתִּי אֶת עֵץ הַצֶּאֱלוֹן נִדְרָךְ בַּקַּיִץ
שֶׁל שְׁדֵרוֹת,
אַדֶּמֶת קְטִיפָתוֹ גַּם הִיא
אֵשׁ רְצוּעָה.

דָּבָר אֵינוֹ נֶחְרָךְ, לֹא הָעוֹר,
הָרְאִיָּה: לְכָאן בָּאנוּ, כַּף
יָדִי הַמְּזִיעָה צְבוּתָה
בְּכַף יָדֵךְ.

וְכָאן הוֹשַׁבְתְּ אוֹתִי מוּל
הַסְּפָרִים. צַמָּה הָיְתָה לָךְ,
הָיוּ עֵינַיִךְ, וְלֹא יָדַעְתִּ
כַּמָּה אַתְּ כְּבָר
גְּאוּלָה.

בַּת שְׁלוֹשׁ־עֶשְׂרֵה, שְׁלוּחָה
מִן הַבָּשָׂר, נוֹשֶׁמֶת אֲוִיר אֲשֶׁר
טִיבוֹ עָלוּם. וְהָעוֹלָם
נִרְעַד, הָעוֹלָם סָאַן, תְּנוּפוֹת שֶׁל אוֹר
כִּרְכָּבִים. תָּפַסְתִּ
אֶת הַתְּנוּעָה, אֶת הַבִּתּוּר, נָשָׂאת

your eyes but horizon there was none,
cranes of warblers lashed the ground,
and dandelion scaffolds
cling, reaching where.

Thirty years you lingered in the here. Walked with us
a touch at most, almost
never tempted by the human din. We in the profanum vulgus
racing through urban sprawl, crossing seas –
Paris, Florence, London, a bundle of appalling flesh and marble, which did not
cease with your cessation

and you're with us, at our side, in your here, craving
love, casting sentences over the distance,
but never shackled.

We knew you utterly without knowing
one fraction. If redemption is losing
the self, then who is
the redeemed.

מַבָּט וְאֹפֶק לֹא הָיָה,
עֲגוּרָנִים שֶׁל פָּשׁוּשִׁים צָלְפוּ בְּתַחְתִּיּוֹת
וּפִגּוּמֵי שֵׁן הָאָרֵי
נֶאֱחָזִים, עוֹלִים לְאָן.

שְׁלוֹשִׁים שָׁנָה נוֹתַרְתִּ בַּכָּאן. הָלַכְתִּ אִתָּנוּ
רַק מְעַט, כְּמְעַט
וְלֹא נִפְתֵּית לְרַחַשׁ הָאֱנוֹשׁ. אֲנַחְנוּ בַּפְּרוֹפָנוּם וּוֹלְגוּס
שָׁעַטְנוּ בַּכְּרַכִּים, חָצִינוּ אֶת הַיָּם –
פָּרִיז, פִּירֶנֶצֶה, לוֹנְדוֹן, גְּבוּבִים שֶׁל גּוּף וְשַׁיִשׁ נִתְעָבִים, שֶׁלֹּא
חָדְלוּ עִם הֶחָדְלֵךְ

וְאַתְּ אִתָּנוּ, מִן הַצַּד, בַּכָּאן שֶׁלָּךְ, שׁוֹעָה
לָאַהֲבָה, מוֹתַחַת מִשְׁפָּטִים עַל הַמֶּרְחָק,
אֲבָל לֹא אֲסוּרָה.

הִכַּרְנוּ אֶת כֻּלֵּךְ בְּלִי לְהַכִּיר שׁוּם
פְּרָט. אִם גְּאֻלָּה הִיא אָבְדָנוֹ
שֶׁל הָעַצְמִי, מִי
זֶה שֶׁנִּגְאָל.

23.

Fine as sea amidst a summered winter
swarms of sun stream into
the stir

Fine as a dim ascent, the stab
of crows across a streetlight,
battered

Fine as a galvanized fence
cutting down the shoreline of
Jaffa

Fine as the word fine
in the flea market, clamoring against
an iron shield

Fine as a polished blade
at home, like the coiled
step walking towards it

כג.

דַּקָּה כְּמוֹ יָם בְּחֹרֶף מְקֻיָּץ
וּנְחִילֵי חַמָּה שׁוֹטְפִים אֶל
הַתְּנוּעָה

דַּקָּה כְּמוֹ נְסִיקָה כֵּהָה, דְּקִירַת
עוֹרֵב מֵעַל פָּנַס רְחוֹב
חָבוּל

דַּקָּה כְּמוֹ מָסַךְ פַּח מְגֻלְוָן
כּוֹרֵת בְּקַו הַחוֹף שֶׁל
יָפוֹ

דַּקָּה כְּמוֹ הַמִּלָּה דַּקָּה
בְּשׁוּק הַפִּשְׁפְּשִׁים, מֻרְעֶשֶׁת מוּל
מָגֵן בַּרְזֶל

דַּקָּה כְּמוֹ לַהַב
הַלָּטוּשׁ בַּבַּיִת, כְּמוֹ צַעַד
הַקָּפוּץ בַּהֲלִיכָה אֵלָיו

Finest of
the fine, fine as a threshold,
as a cut of fear that I might

join
the legions whose grief
turns to bitterness over their own demise.

דַּקָּה מִן
הַדַּקָּה, דַּקָּה כְּמוֹ מִפְּתָן,
כְּמוֹ חִתּוּךְ אֵימָה שֶׁמָּא

אֶפְסַע
אֶל לִגְיוֹנוֹת שֶׁלֶּכֶת אֲהוּבָם
הָיְתָה לִמְרֵרָה עַל אָבְדָנָם שֶׁלָּם.

24.

Noooooo, pain, don't let go—my heart, don't cease in sorrow,

blood, boil, flare, murmur

and body, burn, burn, the nerves winding through the flesh, and you too muscles,

catch fire, bones chafing the innards,

pinch, scratch them some, so that abscess will emerge

thus I shall not ask where her memory is—what oblivion might mime,

thus I shall not let slip between my hands

a sister into time.

כד.

לאאאאאא, אַל תַּרְפֶּה כְּאֵב, לִבִּי, אַל תַּעֲמֹד מִצַּעַר,
דָּם לְהַט, רְתַח, אֵוֵשׁ
וְגוּף, בְּעַר, בְּעַר, הָעֲצַבִּים הַמִּשְׁתָּרְגִים לְאֹרֶךְ הַבָּשָׂר, וְגַם אַתֶּם שְׁרִירִים,
עֲלוּ בָּאֵשׁ, הָעֲצָמוֹת הַמִּתְחַכְּכוֹת בָּאֵיבָרִים הַפְּנִימִיִּים,
דִּקְרוּ, גָּרְדוּ בָּהֶם מְעַט וְתַעֲלֶה מָרְסָה
וּבַל אֶשְׁאַל הֵיכָן זִכְרָהּ, שִׁכְחָתָהּ אֵי אָן
בַּל אֶשְׁמֹט מִבֵּין יָדַי
אָחוֹת אֶל תּוֹךְ הַזְּמַן.

25.

Here you are. Revealed to me molded in the flesh
of Patti Smith, ancient eyes
of poetry, a throat chafed with dust,
time woven from sleep.

Over the pulse
of Tel Aviv and Jaffa, whose electrum
wanes and they have voice: in the bus
I am asked, where is His Glory's place? A hellish country, moaning
in the streets, Cyprus wine, Karshina lye,
why are they used, asks the merchant,
and the neighbor rants unaware in Arabic
Wu'natalti ruha u'shmait batrai kal zia sagi—

Resting in center-sky
a living creature named Aviva, and your forehead
carved with words. A galaxy gliding
through like a fleet of spaceships,
in inverted brightness, like platelets drowning
in a stream of Adolan, they too have melody,
they too sing

כה.

הִנֵּה. נִגְלִית לִי מְכֻיֶּרֶת מִבְּשָׂרָהּ
שֶׁל פָּאטִי סְמִית׳, עֵינַיִם עַתִּיקוֹת
שֶׁל הַשִּׁירָה, גָּרוֹן חָרוּץ עָפָר,
זְמַן קָלוּעַ מִשֵּׁנָה.

מֵעַל לִפְעִימָתָן
שֶׁל תֵּל אָבִיב וְיָפוֹ, שֶׁחַשְׁמַלָּן
נֶחְלַשׁ וְהֵן דּוֹבְרוֹת: בָּאוֹטוֹבּוּס
אֲנִי נִשְׁאָל, אַיֵּה מְקוֹם כְּבוֹדוֹ. וּמִדִּינָהּ שֶׁל גֵּהִנָּם, נֶאֱנָחִים
בָּרְחוֹב, יֵין קַפְּרִיסִין, בּוֹרִית כַּרְשִׁינָה,
לְמָה בָּאִים הַשְּׁנַיִם, נִדְרֶשֶׁת זַבָּנִית,
וְהַשָּׁכֵן הַמִּתְפָּרֵץ פִּתְאוֹם בַּעֲרָבִית
וּנְטָלַתְנִי רוּחָא וּשְׁמָעִית בַּתְרֵי קַל זִיעַ שַׁגִּיא -

עוֹמֶדֶת בְּמֶרְכַּז רָקִיעַ
חַיָּה וּשְׁמֵךְ אֲבִיבָה, וְעַל מִצְחֵךְ
כָּתוּב. גָּלַקְסְיָה מַחְלִיקָה
סָבִיב כְּצִי חֲלָלִיּוֹת
בְּנֹגַהּ מְהֻפָּךְ, כְּטָסִיּוֹת טוֹבְעוֹת
בְּשֶׁטֶף אָדוֹלָן, גַּם לָהֶן שִׁיר,
גַּם הֵן שָׁרוֹת

Birds floundering
between you and the city's brim, till they're scattered
by the hollow voice of your reply,

They leave only a puff behind, a soft stroke
against the windows of my room.
Suddenly I know
what it might mean, to awake
on the shore of dawn,
as light trickles in,
facing the bathroom mirror, pressed for by the body—
you are cold and you are lonely
and there is no angel to cry out in your ear
Arise, Live.

צִפּוֹרִים מְגַשְּׁשׁוֹת
בֵּינֵךְ וּבֵין מִתְאַר הָעִיר, וּנְפוֹצוֹת מֵרִיק הַקּוֹל
שֶׁל תְּשׁוּבָתֵךְ אֵלַי,

נוֹתַר מֵהֶן רַק הֶדֶף, רַק חֲבָטָה רַכָּה
כְּנֶגֶד חַלּוֹנוֹת חַדְרִי.
פִּתְאוֹם אֲנִי יוֹדֵעַ
מָה פֵּרוּשׁוֹ שֶׁל זֶה, לְהִתְעוֹרֵר
עַל שִׂרְטוֹנוֹ שֶׁל שַׁחַר,
בִּדְלִיפָתוֹ שֶׁל אוֹר,
מוּל הָרְאִי בַּשֵּׁרוּתִים, לְהִתָּבַע לַגּוּף -
קַר לָךְ וְאַתְּ בּוֹדֶדָה
וְאֵין מַלְאָךְ שֶׁיִּצְעַק לָךְ בְּאָזְנַיִךְ
קוּמִי וַחֲיִי.

26.

Forty-three years old, you are the woman you will always be.
The forehead still unwrinkled. Your eyes well cradled in their orbits. From
the iris looms a meteoric spark, ramming against the void, slicing
up the space, breaking through a crystalline crust of atmosphere. Amino
acids rush to fuse, hasten to secure their strength. Heavy
mammals step out of the sea, send a famished stare
at the titans of all times. Trees quivering with the thrill, a blazing ball whirling
above them, radiating from its spin the lethal ire, music, a lash
of mercy, ideologies pounding as their wheels of thought go round, a breathless race
whose purpose is just you, in the fatherly heart of broiling *Av.* Heavy heat shatters in air like
splendor, like bones, like fashion. Three and forty years
the light web's bliss cuts your body,
you look with wonder at your feet,
more memory than flesh.

כו.

בַּת אַרְבָּעִים וְשָׁלוֹשׁ, אַתְּ הָאִשָּׁה שֶׁתִּהְיִי כָּל שְׁאַר חַיַּיִךְ.
הַמֵּצַח עוֹד חָלָק. עֵינַיִךְ שְׁקוּעוֹת נָכוֹן בָּאֲרֻבּוֹת. מִתּוֹךְ
הַקַּשְׁתִּיּוֹת נִבָּט שְׁבִיב מֵטֵאוֹר, הַהוּא הַמְנַגֵּשׁ בּוּקָה, חוֹתֵךְ
אֶת הֶחָלָל, מַבְקִיעַ קְרוּם גָּבִישׁ שֶׁל אַטְמוֹסְפֵרָה. חֻמְצוֹת
אָמִינוֹ נֶחְפָּזוֹת לְהִתְרַכֵּב, אָצוֹת אֶל הַבְטָחַת כּוֹחָן. יוֹנְקִים
כְּבֵדִים פּוֹסְעִים הַחוּצָה מִן הַיָּם, נוֹתְנִים מַבָּט מֶרְעָב
בַּעֲנָקֵי הַזְּמַן. עֲצִים מְצֻמְרָרִים מִן הָרִגְשָׁה, כַּדּוּר בּוֹעֵר סְחַרְחַר
מֵעֲלֵיהֶם וּכְבָר קְרוּנוֹת מִסִּיבוּבוֹ חֲמַת הָרֶצַח, מוּסִיקָה, צְלִיפָה
שֶׁל חֶסֶד, אִידֵאוֹלוֹגְיוֹת מוֹעֲכוֹת בְּגַלְגַּלֵּי מַחְשַׁבְתָּן, מֵרוֹץ נִמְהָר
שֶׁתַּכְלִיתוֹ הוּא אַתְּ, בְּלֵב אָב מְרֻתָּח. שָׁרָב שׁוֹבֵר אֶת הָאֲוִיר כְּמוֹ נֵס,
כְּמוֹ עֲצָמוֹת, כְּמוֹ אָפְנָה. שָׁלוֹשׁ וְאַרְבָּעִים שָׁנָה
עֶדְנַת רִשְׁתּוֹת הָאוֹר חוֹרֶצֶת עַל גּוּפֵךְ,
אַתְּ מִסְתַּכֶּלֶת בְּרַגְלַיִךְ בִּתְמִיהָה,
פָּחוֹת בָּשָׂר מִזִּכָּרוֹן.

27.

Her laughter, even a twitch of the lip, the weight
of the earth's foundation
in gold.

What shall encompass them—

Children's sweat, lash of labor, stir
of supply, market fusing in another, columns of
economy, words turning to letters,
electric, pulsing in cyber space

and the world is netted with forces of gravity
of a human kind—

Adar unfolds in melded skies,
a blaze of tungsten
in kitchen knives.

כז.

צְחוֹקָה, אֲפִלּוּ גִּיד שְׂפָתַיִם, מִשְׁקַל
מוֹסְדוֹת הָאָרֶץ
בְּזָהָב.

מָה יְכִילֵם –

זֵעַת הַיְלָדִים, צְלִיפוֹת יִצּוּר, זִיעַ
הַסְּחוֹרָה, שׁוּק מִתְגַּלְגֵּל בְּשׁוּק, וּמְדוֹרֵי
הַכַּלְכָּלָה, מִלִּים הוֹפְכוֹת לְאוֹתִיּוֹת
חַשְׁמַל, דְּפָקִים בְּסַיְבֶּר הֶחָלָל

וְהָעוֹלָם רֹשֵׁת כּוֹחוֹת כְּבִידָה
מִמִּין אֱנוֹשׁ -

אֶדֶר נִפְקַח, רָקִיעַ מְסֻגְסָג זָרַח:
לַהַט טוּנְגְסְטֶן חָסוּם
בְּסַכִּינֵי מִטְבָּח.

28.

Just before I fell asleep I think
I soot right in a language where
I am deft to the pulse of words:
Darkly I roam Sderot city, technobabble with crows,
fragments of Shakespeare, old kings
carry der doters, battlefields, ghosts of the blood
I bump into you. You don't seem to know me
but you are polite, you tell me the time, you give me
directions, confused,
you catch light with sound, you laugh
me off to echoes of morning. Here I am standing
behind poetry-glazed
glass as a self
pounding, pounding, pounding, as you go bye.

כח.

גַ׳סְט בִּיפוֹר אַי פּוֹל אַסְלִיפּ, אַי טִ׳ינְק
אַי שׁוּד וַרְיִט אִין אַ לַנְגְוִיג׳ וֶר
אַי אֶם דֶף טוּ דֶה פּוּלְס אוֹף וּוֹרְדְס:
דַרְקְלִי אַי רוֹאֶם שְׁדֵרוֹת סִיטִי, טֶכְנוֹבַּבֶּלְד וִיט׳ קְרוֹאוֹס,
פְּרַגְמֶנְטְס אוֹף שֶׁקְספִּיר, אוֹלְד קִינְגְס
קְרִי דֶר דוֹאוֹטֶרְס, בָּטֶלְפִילְדְס, גוֹסְטְס אוֹף דֶה בְּלָד.
אַי בַּמְפּ אִינְטוּ יוּ. יוּ דוֹנְט סִים טוּ נוֹ מִי
בָּט יוּ אָר פּוֹלַיְט, יוּ טֶל מִי דֶה טַיְם, יוּ גִיב מִי
דַיֶרְקְשֶׁנְס, קוֹנְפִיוּזְד,
יוּ קֶץ׳ לַיְט וִיט׳ סָאוּנְד, יוּ לָף
מִי אוֹף טוּ אֶקוֹס אוֹף מוֹרְנִינְג הִיר אַי אֶם סְטַנְדִינְג
בִּיהַיְנְד פּוֹאֶטְרִי־גְלֵיזְד
גְלַסְד אָז אָ סֶלְף
פָּאוּנְדִינְג, פָּאוּנְדִינְג, פָּאוּנְדִינְג, אָז יוּ גוֹ בַּי.

It was once already
said— no!

ever since the wind was hung
upon the willows

and objects are devoured by their
calm:

the sun extinguished since its wick was spared,
making charcoal and harm.

(unhand, 3)

פַּעַם נֶאֱמַר
כְּבָר – לֹא!

מֵאָז עַל עֲרָבִים
תְּלוּיָה הָרוּחַ

וַחֲפָצִים טוֹרֵף
הִשָּׁאֵרָם:

הַשֶּׁמֶשׁ הַשָּׁחוּט עַל פְּתִילָתוֹ שֶׁחָסוֹ
וְהוּא עוֹשֶׂה פֶּחָם.

(עֵזֹב, 3)

29.

We were sentenced to be haunted all our days by the tree of the Jews,
that the skies would be shattered by its form,
that beneath the suns—such an exquisite circuit, such a tide of brightness—
its pungency would storm—

What is the scent of memory if not the scent of mourning.
In our veins a nation dreading swamps, addicted to
the dust, whose yearning is twofold:

peace and vengeance;
now we've learned what it is that binds them
into one.

כט.

נִגְזַר לָנוּ שֶׁהַיָּמִים יִהְיוּ מְרֻדָּפִים בְּעֵץ הַיְּהוּדִים,
שֶׁהַשָּׁמַיִם יִשָּׁבְרוּ בְּצוּרָתוֹ,
שֶׁתַּחַת לַשְּׁמָשׁוֹת – סִיבּוּב עָנֹג כָּזֶה, גֵּאוּת כָּזוֹ שֶׁל זֹהַר -
תָּבוֹא חֲרִיפוּתוֹ -

מָה נִיחוֹחוֹ שֶׁל זִכָּרוֹן אִם לֹא נִיחוֹחַ אֵבֶל.
בְּעוֹרְקֵינוּ עַם יֵרֵא בִּצּוֹת, מָכוּר אֶל
הֶעָפָר, שֶׁתְּשׁוּקָתוֹ הִיא שְׁתַּיִם:

שָׁלוֹם וּנְקָמָה;
עַתָּה לָמַדְנוּ אִי זֶה הַדָּבָר הַמַּכְפִּיפָן
בְּיַחַד.

30.

The sons' lot the same as
their fathers', same faces

standing, waiting on the sidewalk.
Time will befall them in cars,
in removing and returning
Torah scrolls, in the cypress' wind.

Qassam rockets will roar as they migrate
north. Spring reflected
in scum upon the water,
in tar,
wax

suddenly the skin is furrowed,
dwindled like nakedness
the sex,
where was it, the street has taken away, taken where,
curse and awe

weighed down their tongues like
coins.

ל.

לַבָּנִים אוֹתוֹ גוֹרָל כְּמוֹ
לָאָבוֹת, אוֹתָם פָּנִים

עוֹמְדִים וּמְחַכִּים עַל מִדְרָכָה.
הַזְּמַן יִקְרֶה לָהֶם בִּמְכוֹנִיּוֹת,
בְּהַכְנָסָה וְהוֹצָאַת סִפְרֵי
תּוֹרָה, בְּרוּחַ בַּבְּרוֹשִׁים.

קָסָמִים יֵהֵמוּ בִּנְדִידָתָם אֶל
הַצָּפוֹן. אָבִיב דּוֹלֵק
בִּירוֹקָה עַל פְּנֵי הַמַּיִם,
בְּזֶפֶת,
שַׁעֲוָה

פִּתְאוֹם הָעוֹר חָרוּשׁ, הַמִּין דָּלִיל
כְּמוֹ עֶרְוָה,
אֵיפֹה הָיָה, הָרְחוֹב לָקַח לְאָן לָקַח,
קְלָלָה וְתַדְהֵמָה

כָּבְדוּ עַל לְשׁוֹנָם כְּמוֹ
מַטְבְּעוֹת.

31.

(Who would we have been if not dispersed, people
who don't ponder their collapse, in the synagogue always at home, fluent
in their language, rolled up in a purified body,
become one with it, who go home to find it there.
No, no going back, there's no return—
concrete existence.

No, it is not time that's crushed between the fingers, the burden of the lands of *Rephaim*;
nor poignant sweetness—a fist's distance parting earth and sky,
Adar crouches on the lawn like law, scarlet pimpernels
stripped bare, the promised rain is dammed
over the neem trees, charging up their growth.
In the streets adolescents pass in a daze,
and when the bombs grow silent
a group of *Bnei Akiva* craze
like Palestinians
on their
roof.)

לא.

(אִלְמָלֵא נִפְצוּנוּ מִי הָיִינוּ, אֲנָשִׁים
שֶׁלֹּא תּוֹהִים עַל נִפּוּצָם. בְּבֵית הַכְּנֶסֶת לֹא חוֹרְגִים, יוֹדְעִים
אֶת הַשָּׂפָה, גְּלוּלִים בַּגּוּף הַמְּחֻטָּא
מְגֻלְגָּלִים אֵלָיו, חוֹזְרִים הַבַּיְתָה וְיֵשְׁנוּ.
לֹא, לֹא חוֹזְרִים, אֵין חֲזָרָה -
קִיּוּם מַמָּשׁ.

לֹא זְמַן נִפְרָדְ בָּאֶצְבָּעוֹת, מַשָּׂא אַרְצוֹת הָרְפָאִים; לֹא נֹעַם
עַז – מֶרְחַק אֶגְרוֹף בֵּין הַשָּׁמַיִם לָרִצְפָּה, אֲדָר רוֹבֵץ
עַל דְּשָׁאִים כְּמוֹ דִּין, מַרְגָּנִיּוֹת קְרוּחוֹת, הַגֶּשֶׁם
הַמְּבֻטָּח סָכוּר מֵעַל אִזְדָּרְכוֹת, טוֹעֵן אֶת
צִמִּיחָתָן. בָּרְחוֹבוֹת הַנְּעוּרִים נָעִים,
שׁוּרָה שֶׁל בְּנֵי עֲקִיבָא בְּשַׁגָּם
בְּשֹׂדְ קָסָאמִים מְרַקְּדִים
כְּפָלַסְטִינִים עַל
גַּגָּם.)

32.

So where is the gate
in Gaza,
in Sderot—

The underworld of former times; the air
still faint
and we go through.

לב.

אָז הֵיכָן הוּא הַשַּׁעַר
בְּעַזָּה,
בִּשְׁדֵרוֹת -

עוֹלַם הַמֵּתִים שֶׁל פַּעַם; הָאֵוִיר
עוֹד דַּק
וַאֲנַחְנוּ עוֹבְרִים.

33.

For years I had this somber velvet
plunged between myself and forces shifting in the dark.

trapped within the synagogue till noon, vein-igniting purity,
then stepping out into the yard, an imposing ficus reigns

in stores of shade, among the foliage,
celestial voices chirp

in the thicket animals pass by, in the gaps
between the shuttered walls, three walls.

At dusk, when Sabbath ended,
my sister would bequeath me books, with fervent soul

I followed, little Sherlock Holmeses
run around with razored minds, slicing

piece by piece. For them, the body's devastation
is a departure point, a reason to entwine, to meld

the loved one's endlessness
into one deduction, all those branchings-out

לג.

שָׁנִים הָיְתָה לִי הַקְּטִיפָה הַזּוֹ, כֵּהָה,
צְנוּחָה בֵּינִי וּבֵין כּוֹחוֹת זָעִים בַּחֹשֶׁךְ.

בְּבֵית הַכְּנֶסֶת סָגוּף עַד צָהֳרַיִם, טֹהַר מְלַקֵּחַ עוֹרְקִים,
וְאָז יוֹצֵא אֶל הֶחָצֵר, פִּיקוּס אֵימְתָנִי חוֹלֵשׁ

בִּמְגוּרוֹת שֶׁל צֵל, בֵּינוֹת לָעֲפָאִים
מְשֻׁרְבָּבוֹת בְּנוֹת קוֹל, מְצַפְצְפוֹת

בְּתוֹךְ הַסְּבַךְ חוֹלְפוֹת חַיּוֹת, בָּרְוָחִים
בֵּין הַחוֹמוֹת הַמּוּגָפוֹת, שָׁלוֹשׁ חוֹמוֹת.

בָּעֲרָבִים, בְּצֵאת הַשַּׁבָּתוֹת צִוְּתָה לִי
אֲחוֹתִי סְפָרִים, בְּנֶפֶשׁ מְאֻמָּץ

אֲנִי עוֹקֵב, הַשֶּׁרְלוֹק הוֹלְמְסִים הַקְּטַנִּים
מִתְרוֹצְצִים עִם שֵׂכֶל מְתֹעָר, חוֹתְכִים

דָּבָר דָּבָר. לָהֶם כִּלְיוֹן הַגּוּף הוּא נְקֻדַּת
מוֹצָא, סִבָּה לִמְשֹׁךְ יַחְדָּו, לִמְסֹךְ

אֶת אֵינְסוֹפוֹ שֶׁל הָאָהוּב
לְתוֹךְ הֶקֵּשׁ אֶחָד, אֶת כָּל הַהִתְפָּרְדוּת

into one event, the smallest of the deeds,
sleep and awakenings, the incense of routine, a gaze

not wholly solved and thus awaits opaque
for resolution, kissed or untouched lips, spells

still singe their rims and the head trembles with bliss. And they were
right: God, death, a machine on space's border

were placed in ashen skies, the legions
of the stars above also followed with their eyes;

As for me, I did not notice their hum, or the flicker, or the drum
of the light's horses who hasten as they summon

the messengers, the pile of evidence—
the darkness beaten over Gaza, chiseled

pipes, gunpowder packed,
Tearing down the veil Sderot.

לְהִתְרַחֲשׁוּת, גּוֹנֵי גּוֹנָם שֶׁל מַעֲשִׂים,
שֵׁנָה וִיקִיצוֹת, קְטֹרֶת הַיּוֹמְיוֹם, מַבָּט

שֶׁלֹּא פָּעֲנַח עַד תֹּם וְהוּא מַמְתִּין אָטוּם
לְגִלּוּיוֹ, שְׂפָתַיִם שֶׁנָּשְׁקוּ אוֹ לֹא נָגְעוּ, לַחַשׁ

עוֹד חוֹרֵךְ אֶת שׁוּלֵיהֶן וְרֹאשׁ רוֹטֵט חֶמְדָּה. וּבֶאֱמֶת
צָדְקוּ: אֱלֹהִים, מָוֶת, מְכוֹנָה עַל גְּבוּל חִיצוֹן

הֻנְּחוּ בְּתוֹךְ שְׁחָקִים מַאֲפִירִים, גַּם לִגְיוֹנוֹת
הַמְּאוֹרוֹת בָּלְשׁוּ מִתּוֹךְ חֹרִים;

לֵב לֹא נָתַתִּי אֲנִי לִזְמִזּוּמָם, וְלָרִצּוּד, לִנְקִישַׁת
סוּסֵי הַנְּהָרָה הַמְּחִישִׁים בַּהֲחִישָׁם

אֶת הַשְּׁלִיחִים, אֶת עֲרֵמַת הָרְאָיוֹת -
הָעֲלָטָה הַחֲבוּטָה עַל עַזָּה, הַצִּנּוֹרוֹת

הַחֲרוּטִים, דְּחוּסִים אֲבַק שְׂרֵפָה,
פּוֹרְמִים אֶת הַפַּרְגּוֹד שְׁדֵרוֹת.

34.

In the year nineteen eighty-seven
I thought the end of the world
was near,
with the sun opaque as the gaze
of a porn star (what was it—
the pleasure? the apathy of heroin?) and summer,
in my memories, eternal
summer

they aired a reality
show: who wants
to plunge down into
the ruse of electricity, the sapphires,
the sharp ice anointed into shapes

and the American, the conqueror of moons,
fixed his binoculars on me, a painful lens,
the neighborhood's cars
howled, birds on the run,
the blind seraph in Sderot's intersection
spewed out: what's wrong with you lately

לד.

בִּשְׁנַת אֶלֶף תְּשַׁע מֵאוֹת שְׁמוֹנִים וְשֶׁבַע
חָשַׁבְתִּי שֶׁסּוֹף הָעוֹלָם
כְּבָר קָרוֹב,
עִם שֶׁמֶשׁ אָטוּם כְּמוֹ מַבָּט
שֶׁל כּוֹכֶבֶת פּוֹרְנוֹ (מָה הָיָה זֶה –
הָעֹנֶג? קְהוּת הַרוֹאִין?) וְקַיִץ,
בְּזִכְרוֹנוֹתַי קַיִץ
תָּמִיד

בַּטֵּלֶוִיזְיָה שֶׁדְּרָה
תָּכְנִית מְציאוּת: מִי רוֹצֶה
לָרֶדֶת אֶל בֵּין
תַּחְבּוּלוֹת הַחַשְׁמַל, סַפִּירִים,
קֶרַח חַד חָבוּר כִּמְשִׁיחָה

וְהָאָמֶרִיקָאִי כּוֹבֵשׁ הַיַּרְחִים
לָטַשׁ בִּי מִשְׁקֶפֶת, עֲדָשָׁה מַכְאִיבָה,
רִכְבֵי הַשְּׁכוּנָה
יִלְּלוּ, צִפּוֹרִים אֲנוּסוֹת,
הַשָּׁרָף הָעִוֵּר שֶׁבְּצֹמֶת שְׁדֵרוֹת
רָשַׁף מָה אִתְּךָ, בַּזְּמַן הָאַחֲרוֹן

you're never home when I call

a lovely curse lay on my lips
and my father clawed my tongue
but dad, I said,
being who I am,
human and limited and mortal,
any attribute of grace is lacking
from my body
in the year of nineteen eighty-seven

and the halt is so quick to arrive.

אַתָּה אַף פַּעַם לֹא בַּבַּיִת
כְּשֶׁאֲנִי מִתְקַשֵּׁר

קַטְרוּג יְפֵהפֶּה הֻנַּח עַל שְׂפָתַי
וְאָבִי אָחַז בִּצְבָת לְשׁוֹנִי,
אֲבָל אַבָּא, אָמַרְתִּי,
מֵעֶצֶם מִי שֶׁאֲנִי
אֱנוֹשִׁי וּמֻגְבָּל וּבֶן מָוֶת
כָּל מִדָּה שֶׁל חֶסֶד נְטוּלָה
מִגּוּפִי
בִּשְׁנַת אֶלֶף תְּשַׁע מֵאוֹת שְׁמוֹנִים וְשֶׁבַע

וְהַדֹּם מְמַהֵר כֹּה לָבוֹא.

35.

Pillars of thistle in the storm's electric bright
only thus might I capture
Adar

A body pierced by fine pins, flame
falling from the heavens, touch anchored
in the void

Friday's dusk, between the days,
will finally be settled
guilt made of guilt

לה.

עַמּוּדֵי בַּרְקָן בְּחַשְׁמַל הַסּוּפָה
רַק כָּךְ אֶפְשָׁר שֶׁאָצוּד אֶת
אֲדָר

גּוּף נָקוּב בְּחֻדִּים, לַהַט
מָט מֵרְקִיעִים, הַמַּגָּע הֶעָגוּן
עַל בְּלִימָה

יוֹם שִׁשִּׁי בֵּין שְׁמָשׁוֹת
יֵרָשֵׁם לְבַסּוֹף
אַשְׁמָה עֲשׂוּיָה בְּאַשְׁמָה

36.

For one day I will desert that city-far-off,
that needle-like pleasure, that desert.
If only nerves of daylight would dart into the heavens' vault
like wounds budding from a wasp's sting
on the day I depart from far-off
to make out of myself a man
who I will fail, time and again,
to make my own.

לו.

כִּי יוֹם אֶחָד אֲנִי עוֹרֵק מֵעִיר־שַׁמָּה,
מִתַּעֲנוּג עַרְעַר, מֵעֲרָבָה.
לוּ יַעַמְדוּ בָּרְקִיעִים עֲצַבֵּי שֶׁמֶשׁ
כַּעֲפָצִים עוֹלִים מֵעֲקִיצַת צִרְעָה
בַּיּוֹם הַזֶּה שֶׁבּוֹ אֲנִי עוֹזֵב אֶת שָׁם
עוֹשֶׂה עַצְמִי אָדָם
שֶׁכָּל חַיַּי יִקְשֶׁה לִי
לִנְשֹׁמוֹ.

37.

Sex and loneliness and coals
stars of coal,
black cries, the economy of crows,
speckling them with holes.

The nail in the hand, the nail in the head,
the wreckage of darkness and teeth marks of words.
In the morning, once more, I did not know what should be done with the blood—
it moves from me to the world in a flood.

לז.

מִין וּבְדִידוּת וּפֶחָם,
כּוֹכָבִים שֶׁל פֶּחָם,
זְעָקוֹת שְׁחוֹרוֹת, כַּלְכָּלַת הָעוֹרְבִים
הַנּוֹקְרִים בְּתוֹכָם.

הַמַּסְמֵר שֶׁבַּיָּד, הַמַּסְמֵר שֶׁבָּרֹאשׁ,
שֶׁבֶּר הַחֹשֶׁךְ וּנְשִׁיכַת הַמִּלָּה.
בַּבֹּקֶר שׁוּב לֹא יָדַעְתִּי מָה יֵעָשֶׂה עִם הַדָּם -
זֶה עוֹזֵב אוֹתִי וְהוֹלֵךְ לָעוֹלָם.

38.

Like lovers who house-warmed by fucking
in every corner, madness
thrust against the walls, on the counter, trapped
in kitchen drawers,
I too cried for Tel Aviv:

This saltiness will not swerve
from the ficus trees, from these skies
enrobing themselves in *Tevet* like a young nude
exposed in mid-shower.

And the smell of tearing flesh
will cling to the sidewalks, to the climbing prices
of apartments, to those beasts on their bicycles
sparing themselves on the seashore,

to the relentless pulse
of wireless transmission.
Your whitened blood will shoot its arrow—
And I'll deliver into ruin that city of extremes
hater of the poor, of the lonely,
of the pursuer of
dreams.

לח.

כָּאוֹהֲבִים אֲשֶׁר חָנְכוּ בֵּיתָם בְּזִיּוּנִים
בְּכָל פִּנָּה, פִּרְאוּת
מוּטַחַת בַּכְּתָלִים, בַּשַּׁיִשׁ, תְּפוּסָה בִּמְגֵרוֹת
מִטְבָּח,
בָּכִיתִי גַּם אֲנִי אֶת תֵּל אָבִיב:

מְלִיחוּת זוֹ לֹא תָּסוּר
מֵעַם הַפִּיקוּסִים, מִן הַשְּׁחָקִים
הַמִּתְכַּסִּים טֵבֵת כְּנַעֲרָה
שֶׁהִתְפָּרְצוּ אֶל מִקְלַחְתָּהּ.

וְרֵיחַ הִקָּרְעוּת בָּשָׂר
יִדְבַּק בַּמִּדְרָכוֹת, בִּמְחִירֵי דִּירוֹת
מַאֲמִירִים, בַּבְּהֵמוֹת הַנּוֹשָׁעִים
בְּאוֹפַנַּיֵּהֶם עַל קַו הַחוֹף,

בַּהֹלֶם
הַנָּחוּשׁ שֶׁל תִּמְסוֹרוֹת אַלְחוּטִיּוֹת.
דָּמֵךְ שֶׁהִיא הִלְבִּינָה שׁוֹט יִקְשֹׁט -
מָסַרְתִּי לְחָרְבָּה אֶת הַקִּרְיָה הַזֹּאת
שׁוֹנֵאת לָעֲנִיִּים, לַגַּלְמוּדִים,
לְבַעֲלֵי
הַחֲלוֹמוֹת.

39.

Sderot is clenched in winter, a radiance of cotton caresses
from above. First the warblers
stiffen to fall,
then bushes glazed with ice
crop up, a whack, chime rings against
the winds, then the engines spin
and rasp, a swish blows past, it is the cypress trees, I think,
flap and flutter, crows laden with moans
across a streetlight. And your voice arrives, no longer lost
in music, no longer sweetened—as from now on
it shall ring, as it had always rung, it is I
who hears its crack
I whose life has been a detour
from your
lack.

לט.

שְׁדֵרוֹת נִקְפֶּצֶת חֹרֶף, קְרִינַת כֶּתְנָה נוֹשֶׁקֶת
מֵרְקִיעִים. תְּחִלָּה הַפָּשׁוֹשִׁים
קְשׁוּיִים לַנְּפִילָה,
אַחַר כָּךְ מִתְגַּשְּׁמִים
שִׂיחִים מְזֻגְּגֵי קָרָה, מַכָּה, דִּנְדּוּן כְּנֶגֶד
הָרוּחוֹת, וְאָז הַמְּנוֹעִים סַבִּים
וְנִחָרִים, וְיֵשׁ רִשְׁרוּשׁ, נִדְמֶה לִי שֶׁבְּרוֹשִׁים
טְפִיחוֹת, טְפִיחוֹת, טְפִיחוֹת, עוֹרְבִים כְּבֵדִים כַּאֲנָחוֹת
עַל פָּנְסֵי רְחוֹב. וּבָא קוֹלֵךְ, לֹא עוֹד אוֹבֵד
בַּנְּגִינָה, לֹא עוֹד נִמְתָּק – כְּפִי
שֶׁיִּהְיֶה מִכָּאן, כְּפִי שֶׁתָּמִיד הִנּוֹ, אֲנִי
הוּא הַשּׁוֹמֵעַ
שֶׁכָּל חַיַּי עַד כָּאן
הָיוּ הֶסֵּחַ שֶׁלֹּא
אֶתְגַּעְגֵּעַ.

40.

I'll probably lose my mind, this dick just doesn't hold
memory oddity identity. Everyone knows to babble something or another
about the fraying, the stutter, as if the GodofDeath
had not yet emerged and were a polished blade, a praising sound of the *Shofar*, behold and you too shall
see, He will leave you nothing but a crevice in the throat through which I
whisper to my sister: take thee a portion of my body that you may live. And to Tel Aviv,
to her I sing afresh: youth bathed in flesh, newspapers soaring on
the city's curse, trade thieving your past and your trees – what have I to do with your Glory
and you with your deeds. It just doesn't hold. And to Sderot I'm thrust
on a chariot of fire to ask the pardon of Tamar, my mother, oh mother, countless times it will befall her,
she will raise her voice and weep, like a maniac I'm running up and down the streets, I'm leaving home
only for the graveyard. And brothers and sisters and nephews and nieces, don't think oh
so hearty, this familial warmth and the simplicity of being. There's only a preachy *Drash* side to this
story, your loved ones make demands, on end, grab you by the hand, you cross the river there
you'll forget, Amen I say, say to whom, why did you allow the miracles to grind your bones
in a decelerated crash. Draining calcium, fractures not yet healed, eroded joints,
it's time, eventually you will adapt to time, your expiration date has passed, mammals flirting on the
estuary of history. Like that sight of boundless splendor I've envisioned in a dream, driving
in an AIL Storm collapsed of its troops, Aviva at my side, in the distance a white tower shouts at the
clouds, *Mitzpe Ramon* I conjecture in her ear, we're heading to Eilat, but no desert is in view, *Kurkar*
sandstones and open lakes resting in their sockets, glinting fish, fowl perhaps, gaped
hibiscus groaning, braying: wake. And I arouse to a morning of ecstatic light.

מ.

קָרוֹב לְוַדַּאי שֶׁאֶשְׁתַּגֵּעַ, לֹא מַחְזִיק הַזַּיִן הַזֶּה
זָרוּת זִכָּרוֹן זֶהוּת. כֻּלָּם יוֹדְעִים לְבַרְבֵּר מַשֶּׁהוּ אֶחָד
עַל הַפְּרָמִים, עַל הַגִּמְגּוּם, כְּאִלּוּ אֱלֹהִימָוֶת
לֹא הֵגִיחַ וְהוּא לַהַב מְמֹרָט, הוּא תֵּקַע שׁוֹפָר, רָאֹה תִּרְאוּ כָּמוֹנִי הוּא יַשְׁאִיר לָכֶם
רַק סֶדֶק בַּגָּרוֹן שֶׁבַּעֲדוֹ אֲנִי
לוֹאֵט אֶל אַחוֹתִי: קְחִי לָךְ הַחֵלֶק מִגּוּפִי וַחֲיִי מִמֶּנּוּ לְמַעַן תִּחְיִי. וּלְתֵל אָבִיב
לָהּ אֲנִי שָׁר: הַנְּעוּרִים הַנִּרְחָצִים בָּשָׂר, הָעִתּוֹנִים הַמַּגְבִּיהִים אֲוִיר עַל
תַּאֲלַת הָעִיר, הַמִּסְחָר הַמְגַנֵּב אֶת עֲבָרֵךְ וְאֶת עֲצִיבֵךְ – לָמָּה לִי תְּהִלָּתֵךְ
וְלָמָּה לָךְ יָמַיִךְ. זֶה לֹא מַחְזִיק. וְלִשְׁדֵרוֹת אֲנִי נִרְחָף
בְּרֶכֶב אֵשׁ לְחַלּוֹת פְּנֵי תָּמָר, אִמִּי, אִמִּי, אֵינְסְפּוֹר פְּעָמִים יִקָּרֶה לָהּ,
הִיא תֵּבְךְ, אֲנִי יָרוּץ כְּמוֹ מְטֹרֶפֶת בָּרְחוֹבוֹת, מֵהַבַּיִת אֲנִי
יִצֵּא רַק לְבֵית הָעָלְמִין. וְאַחִים וַאֲחָיוֹת וְאַחְיָנִים אַחְיָנִיּוֹת, אַל תַּחְשְׁבוּ כַּמָּה חָמִים, אָה,
הַחֲמִימוּת הַמִּשְׁפַּחְתִּית הַזֹּאת, וּפַשְׁטוּתוֹ שֶׁל הַקִּיּוּם. רַק דְּרָשׁ יֵשׁ בַּסִּפּוּר, אֲהוּבֵיכֶם דּוֹרְשִׁים
אֶתְכֶם, קַו לָקָו, לוֹקְחִים אֶתְכֶם בַּיָּד, אַתֶּם חוֹצִים אֶת הַנָּהָר שָׁם
תִּשְׁכְּחוּ, אָמֵן אֲנִי אוֹמֵר לָכֶם, לְמִי אֲנִי אוֹמֵר, לָמָּה הִנַּחְתֶּם לַנִּסִּים לִמְחֹץ עַצְמוֹתֵיכֶם
בְּהִתְרַסְּקוּת מוּאֶטֶת. סִידָן דּוֹלֵף, שְׁבָרִים שֶׁלֹּא הֶחְלִימוּ עַד תֻּמָּם, שְׁחוּקִים הַמִּפְרָקִים,
הִגִּיעַ זְמַן, לַזְּמַן כְּבָר תִּתְרַגְּלוּ, כְּבָר נִפְגְּתֶם, יוֹנְקִים עוֹגְבִים עַל
שֶׁפֶךְ הַהִיסְטוֹרִיָּה. כַּמַּחֲזֶה אֲשֶׁר חָזִיתִי בַּחֲלוֹם יִפִּי אֵין שִׁעוּר לוֹ, נוֹהֵג בְּתוֹךְ סוּפָה
הַמִּתְכַּלָּה מֵחֲלִיָּתָהּ, אֲבִיבָה לְצִדִּי, בַּמֶּרְחַקִּים מִגְדָּל לָבָן צָעוּק אֶל עֲנָנִים, מִצְפֵּה רָמוֹן
שֵׁעַרְתִּי בְּאָזְנָה, אֲנַחְנוּ בַּדֶּרֶךְ לְאֵילַת, וְאֵין מִדְבָּר, צְבִירֵי כֶּרְכֶּר וַאֲגַמִּים פְּתוּחִים
בְּשִׁקְעֵיהֶם, דָּגִים מְבֹהָקִים, סָפֵק עוֹפוֹת, הִיבִּיסְקוּסִים פְּעוּרֵי
לֹעוֹת מְנָאֲקִים וְנוֹעֲרִים לִי עוֹר. אֲנִי נֵעוֹר אֶל בֹּקֶר מְרֻגָּשׁ מֵאוֹד.

One can claim eternity is this, I told my mother
and she replied, both of us caught in the congealment of all brightness, we did not utter her name
lest we burst, just like at nights when my mind turns to glass, on the verge of pounding
against the skull. But of factories destroyed by barren shooting we spoke. We pawned
another hour of ourselves in that way, Amen I tell you, this is the secret, to linger is the
essence of it all, like the emergency alert system hindering with a strident murmur
the movement of bombs alive with fire.

אֶפְשָׁר לִטְעוֹן שֶׁזֶּה הַנֶּצַח, אָמַרְתִּי לְאִמִּי
וְהִיא עָנְתָה, שְׁרוּיִים בְּהִתְקָרְשׁוּת הַזֹּהַר בָּעוֹלָם, אֶת שְׁמָהּ לֹא הֶעֱלֵינוּ פֶּן
נִפְרֹץ, כְּמוֹ בָּעֲרָבִים שֶׁאָז מוֹחִי זְכוּכִית, נִדְמֶה שֶׁהִנֵּה הוּא נִדְפָּק
כְּנֶגֶד הַגֻּלְגֹּלֶת. אֲבָל עַל הֶרֶס מִפְעָלִים מִיְּרִי רֵיק דִּבַּרְנוּ. מִשְׁכַּנּוּ עוֹד שָׁעָה
אֶצְלֵנוּ, אָמַן אֲנִי אוֹמֵר לָכֶם, שֶׁזֶּה הַסּוֹד, מַהוּת הַכֹּל הִתְמַהְמְהוּת, כְּהִסְהוּסָהּ שֶׁל
מַעֲרֶכֶת הַכְּרִיזָה הַמְעַכֶּבֶת בְּגִרְגּוּר צוֹרֵם רָקֵטוֹת לוֹהֲבוֹת.

41.

Orchid, a tree, perhaps
only a bush, and still, a verdant vessel
seizing voices that *Nissan*
threatens to eject: a stamen—a caw of color, a petal—
a howl of hue.
This is all in reach, that is,
unreachable, in Gaza, in Sderot,
an enthralled *Adar* is swarming. Heavy mud,
fowl of all kinds wrack houses with their squalls,
a moon, the heart of day, pillars of dust.
This is all in reach, that is, retracted
from the world, detached from me—
Is this the journey's end?
I am bewildered,
still none the wiser—
And if this is its cusp,
weary as I am, how will I begin

מא.

בּוֹהִינְיָה, עֵץ, אוּלַי
רַק שִׂיחַ, בְּכָל זֹאת, בָּזִיךְ יָרֹק
כּוֹלֵא קוֹלוֹת אֲשֶׁר נִיסָּן גּוֹהֵר
לִפְרֹץ: אַבְקָן – צְנִיפָה שֶׁל צֶבַע, עֲלֵה כּוֹתֶרֶת –
בְּכִי גָּוֵן.
כָּל זֶה מֻשָּׂג, מַשְׁמָע,
בִּלְתִּי מֻשָּׂג, בְּעַזָּה, בִּשְׂדֵרוֹת
רוֹחֵשׁ אֵדֶר אָלֶף. בֹּץ כָּבֵד,
מִינֵי עוֹפוֹת הוֹרְסִים בָּתִּים בְּצוּחָתָם,
יָרֵחַ, לֵב הַיּוֹם, תִּימֹרֶת שֶׁל אָבָק.
כָּל זֶה מֻשָּׂג, מַשְׁמָע מוּסָּג מִן
הָעוֹלָם, נִפְרָד מִמֶּנִּי –
הֲזֶה סוֹפוֹ שֶׁל הַמַּסָּע?
אֲנִי מֻפְתָּע
לֹא הֶחְכַּמְתִּי –
וְאִם סִפּוֹ,
אֲנִי עָיֵף, כֵּיצַד אַתְחִיל

42.

This poem is not fit for music, it reaches from afar,
from a kingdom where no tune is needed.
There's no breaking through from there to darkness
to single handedly recover the shards—

only ghosts once flesh and voice

and the worldly land laden with roads
Sderot-Tel Aviv, Gaza-Sderot, a magnetized
snap on a Strip of tape:

sighs of song in cities pressed by deimos at sundown, an eyeball
slashed as it sees, the possibility is a blade, a little gleaming blade,
Majbed, shidi al ha-shba, sahadi be-za'in
He ridicules from His heavens—
to get up from the shiv'ah on "And Jacob dwelt"
visit the gravesite on "And Jacob lived"

Climb and shake the trees to learn,
do the waters have names? And savor, not an ashen
sting, and go hold sway over the fowl of the air
and every living thing that moves upon the earth,
over that called fire, for example, what heat did you discover there?

מב.

וּמוּסִיקָה לַשִּׁיר הַזֶּה אֵין, מֵרָחוֹק הוּא מַגִּיעַ,
מִמַּלְכוּת אֵין לָהּ צֹרֶךְ בִּצְלִיל.
לֹא הוֹרְסִים מִשָּׁם אֶל הַחֹשֶׁךְ
לְהָשִׁיב בַּיָּד חֲרָסִים –

רַק רִפְאוּת שֶׁהָיְתָה בָּשָׂר וְקוֹלוֹת

וְהָאָרֶץ אַרְצִית חֲרוּצָה בְּצִירִים
שְׁדֵרוֹת־תֵּל אָבִיב, עַזָּה־שְׁדֵרוֹת, פִּצְפּוּץ
מְמֻגְנָט בִּרְצוּעַת הַקְלָטָה:

רַחַשׁ עֲנוֹת, בֶּעָרִים מְעוּכוֹת דִּימוֹסֵי הַזְּרִיחָה, גַּלְגַּל עַיִן
שֶׁסַּף בִּשְׁעַת רְאִיָּה, אֶפְשָׁרוּת הִיא לַהַב, לַהַב קָטָן וְנוֹצֵץ,
מִז'בֶּד, שִׁירִי עַל הַשְּׁבָּה, סַהֲרִי בְּזַיִן
רְקִיעָיו צְחוֹק עָשָׂה –
לִשְׁבֹּת מִן הָאֵבֶל פָּרָשַׁת וַיֵּשֶׁב
לַעֲלוֹת אֶל הַקֶּבֶר פָּרָשַׁת וַיְחִי.

זַעְזְעוּ וְטַפְּסוּ בָּעֵצִים וְגַלּוּ,
יֵשׁ לַמַּיִם שֵׁמוֹת? וְטַעַם, לֹא דֹּק
מְעָפָר, וּרְדוּ לִרְדוֹת בְּחַיַּת הַשָּׂדֶה וּבָעוֹף,
בְּזוֹ הַקְרוּיָה אֵשׁ, לְמָשָׁל, אֵיזֶה חֹם מִצָּאתֶם?

Tell me, though night already offered up his lips
and a mighty moon is wrinkled
in his throat—

Ever since creation ceased, the dead have spoken
in Hebrew:
on 18 *Kislev 5768*,
only inches came between
the toilet seat
and the Seat of Mercy.

אִמְרוּ לִי, אַף שֶׁלַּיְלָה הִגִּישׁ אֶת שְׂפָתָיו
וּלְבָנָה אַדִּירָה קְמוּטָה
בִּגְרוֹנוֹ –

מִיּוֹם שֶׁחָדְלָה הַבְּרִיאָה, דִּבְּרוּ הַמֵּתִים
בְּעִבְרִית:
יוֹד חֵית בְּכִסְלֵו הַתַּשְׂסַח
סַנְטִים מַחְרִיד
אֶת בֵּית הַכִּסֵּא
מִכִּסֵּא הַכָּבוֹד.

43.

A psalm for Tamar may you be saved from the ashes
from ashen days and ashen dust
and if in this life there is a life beyond the life of the body
may you have it
and may you be kept from the temptation to hover once again with him, the drunkard
your heart for his heart, your tongue for his tongue
before the first word is uttered

Sderot, Tel Aviv Jaffa
25 Kislev – Rosh Chodesh Adar II, 5768

מג.

מִזְמוֹר לְתָמָר יוֹשִׁיעוּךְ מִן הָאֵפֶר
מִיָּמִים שֶׁל אֵפֶר מִן הָאֵפֶר גַּם
וְאִם יֵשׁ בְּחַיִּים אֵלֶּה חַיִּים מֵעֵבֶר לְחַיֵּי הַגּוּף
יִתְּנוּךְ אוֹתָם
וְיִשְׁמְרוּךְ מִן הַפִּתּוּי לָשׁוּב אֶל הָרְחִיפָה אִתּוֹ־שִׁכּוֹר
לִבֵּךְ תַּחַת לִבּוֹ שְׂפָתָיו תַּחַת שְׂפָתֵךְ
בְּטֶרֶם תֵּאָמֵר הַמִּלָּה הָרִאשׁוֹנָה

שדרות, תל אביב יפו
כ"ה כסלו – ר"ח אדר ב', התשס"ח

Recent Titles from Alice James Books

Half/Life: New & Selected Poems, Jeffrey Thomson
Odes to Lithium, Shira Erlichman
Here All Night, Jill McDonough
To the Wren: Collected & New Poems, Jane Mead
Angel Bones, Ilyse Kusnetz
Monsters I Have Been, Kenji C. Liu
Soft Science, Franny Choi
Bicycle in a Ransacked City: An Elegy, Andrés Cerpa
Anaphora, Kevin Goodan
Ghost, like a Place, Iain Haley Pollock
Isako Isako, Mia Ayumi Malhotra
Of Marriage, Nicole Cooley
The English Boat, Donald Revell
We, the Almighty Fires, Anna Rose Welch
DiVida, Monica A. Hand
pray me stay eager, Ellen Doré Watson
Some Say the Lark, Jennifer Chang
Calling a Wolf a Wolf, Kaveh Akbar
We're On: A June Jordan Reader, Edited by Christoph Keller and Jan Heller Levi
Daylily Called It a Dangerous Moment, Alessandra Lynch
Surgical Wing, Kristin Robertson
The Blessing of Dark Water, Elizabeth Lyons
Reaper, Jill McDonough
Madwoman, Shara McCallum
Contradictions in the Design, Matthew Olzmann
House of Water, Matthew Nienow
World of Made and Unmade, Jane Mead
Driving without a License, Janine Joseph
The Big Book of Exit Strategies, Jamaal May
play dead, francine j. harris
Thief in the Interior, Phillip B. Williams
Second Empire, Richie Hofmann
Drought-Adapted Vine, Donald Revell
Refuge/es, Michael Broek
O'Nights, Cecily Parks

Alice James Books is committed to publishing books that matter. The press was founded in 1973 in Boston, Massachusetts as a cooperative, wherein authors performed the day-to-day undertakings of the press. This element remains present today, as authors who publish with the press are invited to collaborate closely in the publication process of their work. AJB remains committed to its founders' original feminist mission, while expanding upon the scope to include all voices and poets who might otherwise go unheard. In keeping with its efforts to build equity and increase inclusivity in publishing and the literary arts, AJB seeks out poets whose writing possesses the range, depth, and ability to cultivate empathy in our world and to dynamically push against silence. The press was named for Alice James, sister to William and Henry, whose extraordinary gift for writing went unrecognized during her lifetime.

Designed by Tiani Kennedy

Printed by McNaughton & Gunn